1000 FACTS ON
ANCIENT HISTORY

First published by Miles Kelly Publishing Ltd
Bardfield Centre, Great Bardfield
Essex, CM7 4SL

2 4 6 8 10 9 7 5 3 1

Editor
Belinda Gallagher

Assistant Editor
Mark Darling

Art Director
Clare Sleven

Designer
Venita Kidwai

Picture Research
Liberty Newton

British Library Cataloguing-in-Publication Data
A catalogue record for this book is available from the British Library

ISBN 1-84236-034-5

Printed in Hong Kong

www.mileskelly.net
info@mileskelly.net

1000 FACTS ON
ANCIENT
HISTORY

John Farndon
Consultant Richard Tames

Miles Kelly
PUBLISHING

Contents

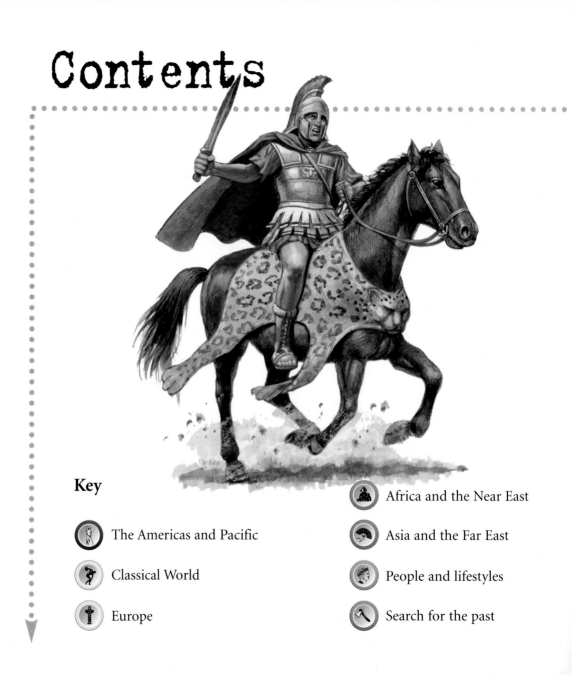

Key

Contents

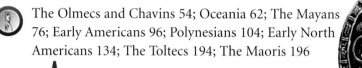

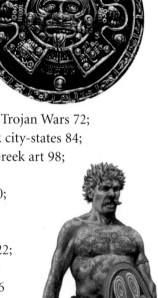

Contents

Contents

Origins of mankind

- **Humans and apes** have so many similarities – such as long arms and fingers, and a big brain – that most experts think they must have evolved from the same creature.

- **The common ancestor** may be four-legged orang-utan-like creatures called dryopithecines that lived in trees 22-10 million years ago, like 'Proconsul' from E. Africa.

- **The break came when** 'hominids' (human-like apes) began to live on the ground and walk on two legs.

- **Footprints** of three bipedal (two-legged) creatures from 4 mya were found preserved in ash at Laetoli, Tanzania.

- **The oldest hominid** is called *Ardipithecus ramidus*, known from 4.4 million years ago bone fragments found in Aramis, Ethiopia.

- **Many very early** hominids are australopiths ('southern apes'), for example, *Australopithecus anamensis* from 4.2 million years ago.

- **Australopiths** were only 1 m tall and their brain was about the same size as an ape's, but they were bipedal.

- **The best known** australopith is 'Lucy', a skeleton of *Australopithecus afarensis* of 3 million years ago, found in Kenya in 1974.

- **Lucy's discoverers** – Don Johanson and Maurice Tieb – called her Lucy because they were listening to the Beatles' song 'Lucy in the Sky with Diamonds' at the time.

- **Many early hominid** remains are just skulls. Lucy was an almost complete skeleton. She showed that hominids learned to walk upright before their brains got bigger.

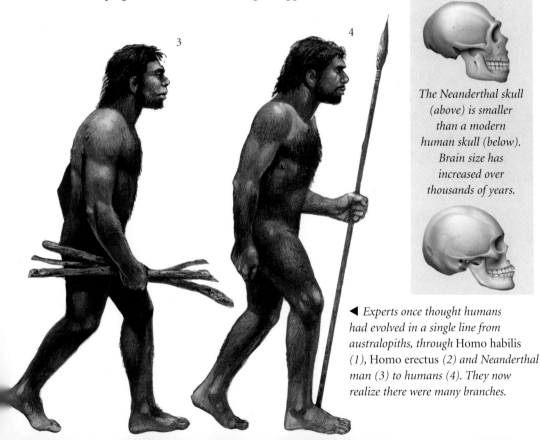

The Neanderthal skull (above) is smaller than a modern human skull (below). Brain size has increased over thousands of years.

◄ Experts once thought humans had evolved in a single line from australopiths, through Homo habilis (1), Homo erectus (2) and Neanderthal man (3) to humans (4). They now realize there were many branches.

9

Handy man

- **2.5-1.8 mya**, the first really human-like hominids appeared. These hominids are all given the genus (group) name *Homo*, and include us.

- **The best known** early Homos are *Homo rudolfensis* and *Homo habilis*.

- **The first** Homos were taller than australopiths and had bigger brains.

- **Unlike australopiths,** Homos ate meat. They may have been forced to eat meat by a drying of the climate that cut the amount of plant food that was available.

- **Brains need** a lot of food, and eating meat gave the extra nourishment that is required for bigger brains.

- *Homo habilis* is known from pieces of hand bones, a jaw and a skull found in Tanzania's Olduvai Gorge in 1961.

▲ Homo habilis *was the first tool-making human. Flint was the most suitable material and flakes were chipped off using a bone hammer. The main piece of flint was shaped into a hand axe. The flakes of flint were used as cutting tools.*

- *Homo habilis* means 'Handy Man'. He gets his name because he has a good grip for wielding tools – with a thumb that can be rotated to meet the tip of a finger. This is called an 'opposable thumb'.

- **The first Homos** used bones or stones to break open bones to get at the nourishing marrow. Later they sharpened stones to cut meat for eating and hides for clothing. They may even have built simple shelters to live in.

10

- **Some experts** think the bulge in 'Broca's area' of certain *Homo habilis* skulls suggests they could speak in a crude way. Most think they could not.

- **The first Homos** lived for a million or more years alongside 'robust' (bigger) australopiths such as *Paranthropus boisei*.

◄ *Skulls that have been found show that the first Homos, like* Homo habilis *shown here, had brains of 650 cubic cm (cc) – twice as big as australopiths. Ours are about 1400 cc. However, they had ape-like faces with protruding jaws and sloping foreheads.*

11

Man, the hunter

- **About 2 mya,** a much taller *Homo* called *Homo ergaster* appeared. Ergasters were the first creatures to have bodies much like ours, with long legs and straight backs.

- **Adult ergasters** were 1.6 m tall, weighed 65 kg and had brains of 850 cubic cm, well over half as big as ours.

- **Ergasters** did not just scavenge for meat like *Homo habilis.* They went hunting for large animals.

- **For hunting** and cutting up meat, ergaster made double-edged blades or 'hand-axes' from pieces of stone, shaping them by chipping off flakes. Experts call this Acheulean tool-making.

- **To hunt** effectively, ergasters had to work together, so co-operation was the key to their success – and may have quickly led to the development of speech.

- **Ergasters** may have painted their bodies with red ochre (a mineral found in the ground).

- **Shortly after** ergaster came *Homo erectus* ('Upright Man').

- **Erectus** remains are found as far from Africa as Java. 700,000-year-old stone tools on the Indonesian island of Flores suggest they may have travelled by boat.

▲ *This teardrop-shaped stone tool is typical of ergaster and* H. erectus.

- **Erectus** learned to light fires, so they could live in colder places, and make a wider range of food edible by cooking.

▼ *As he developed a greater variety of stone tools, early man was more successful at hunting down and eating wild animals.*

...**FASCINATING FACT**...
Long legs and working in groups helped
ergaster to spread beyond Africa into
Asia and maybe Europe.

Later hunters

- **Hominids** appeared in Europe much later. The oldest, called *Homo antecessor*, dates from 800,000 years ago. This may have been a kind of erectus, or another species.

- **800,000-600,000 years ago**, *Homo heidelbergensis* appeared in parts of Europe, Asia and Africa.

- **Heidelbergensis** may be a single species that came from Africa – or various species that evolved in different places.

- *Homo heidelbergensis* has many features in common with *Homo erectus*, but is a major step on the way to modern humans with, for the very first time, a brain as big as ours.

- **Heidelbergensis** made good stone tools by making the core first, then shaping the blade with a single blow.

- **Heidelbergensis** was ancestor to Neanderthal Man, who lived in Europe from 250,000 to 30,000 years ago.

- **Neanderthals** were named after the Neander valley in Germany, where remains were found in 1856.

- **Neanderthals** were slightly shorter than modern humans but much stronger and with bigger brains. They must have been formidable hunters.

- **Neanderthals** buried their dead, often with tributes of flowers.

- **Neanderthals** were living in Croatia 28,000 years ago – long after modern humans had appeared. No one knows why Neanderthal Man died out, leaving humans alone.

▼ *Most early hominid remains have been found in Africa. Many species – including modern humans – may have emerged first in Africa, then migrated elsewhere. These are sites where remains were found.*

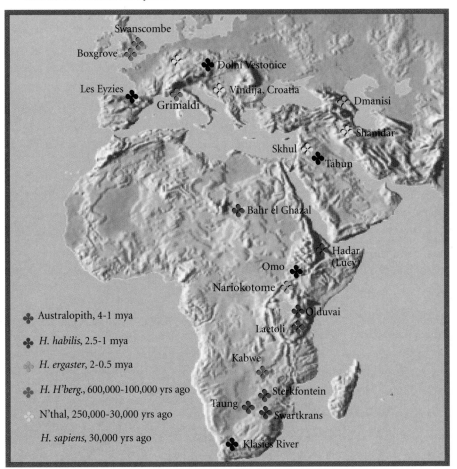

Swanscombe
Boxgrove
Les Eyzies
Grimaldi
Dolni Vestonice
Vindija, Croatia
Dmanisi
Shanidar
Skhul
Tabun
Bahr el Ghazal
Hadar (Lucy)
Omo
Nariokotome
Olduvai
Laetoli
Kabwe
Sterkfontein
Taung
Swartkrans
Klasies River

♣ Australopith, 4-1 mya

♣ *H. habilis*, 2.5-1 mya

♣ *H. ergaster*, 2-0.5 mya

♣ *H. H'berg.*, 600,000-100,000 yrs ago

♣ N'thal, 250,000-30,000 yrs ago

H. sapiens, 30,000 yrs ago

15

Modern humans

- **The scientific name** for modern humans is *Homo sapiens sapiens*. The word *sapiens* is used twice to distinguish us from *Homo sapiens neanderthalis* (Neanderthal Man).

- **Unlike Neanderthals,** modern humans have a prominent chin and a flat face with a high forehead.

- **Some scientists** think that because we all share similar DNA, all humans are descended from a woman nicknamed 'Eve', who they calculate lived in Africa about 200,000 years ago. DNA is the special molecule in every body-cell that carries the body's instructions for life.

- **The oldest human** skulls are 130,000 years old and were found in the Omo Basin in Ethiopia and the Klasies River in South Africa.

- **About 30,000** years ago, modern humans began to spread out into Eurasia from Africa.

- **The earliest** modern Europeans are called Cro-Magnon Man, after the caves in France's Dordogne valley where skeletons from 35,000 years ago were found in 1868.

- **Modern humans** reached Australia by boat from Indonesia 50,000 years ago. They reached the Americas from Asia about the same time.

◄ *Both modern humans and Neanderthals used beautifully made spears for hunting.*

- **Modern humans** lived alongside Neanderthals for tens of thousands of years in the Middle East and Europe.

- **Modern humans** were probably the first creatures to speak what we would call language. Some scientists think language was a sudden genetic 'accident' that remained and developed because it gave humans a huge advantage.

- **With modern** humans came rapid advances in stone-tool technology, the building of wooden huts, a rise in population and a growing interest in art.

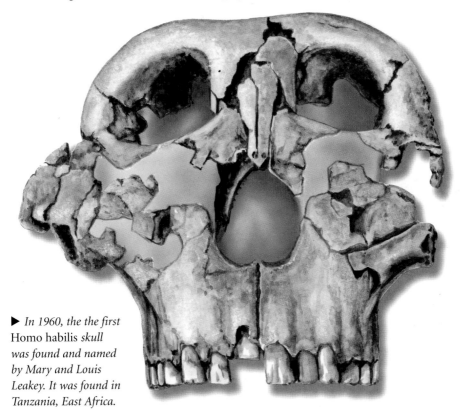

▶ *In 1960, the the first* Homo habilis *skull was found and named by Mary and Louis Leakey. It was found in Tanzania, East Africa.*

Cave painters

- **Prehistoric people** sometimes lived in caves, but more often they went into caves to paint and draw.

- **The world's** most famous cave paintings, at Lascaux in France and Altamira in Spain, were found by children.

- **Carbon** dating shows that the paintings in Lascaux are 31,000 years old. Those in Chauvet in the French Ardèche are nearly twice as old.

- **The pictures** at Cougnac, France, were painted over a period of 10,000 years.

- **Most paintings** in caves show large animals such as bison, deer, horses and mammoths.

- **Caves may** have been the temples of prehistoric times, and the paintings linked to religious rituals.

- **Cave artists** often painted by spitting paint, a practice also followed by the aboriginal people of Australia.

- **To reach the** 14,000-year-old paintings in France's Pergouset, you must crawl through 150 m of passages.

- **In the caves** at Nerja in Spain there are rock formations that prehistoric people played like a xylophone.

- **The aboriginal** paintings on rocks in Arnhemland, Northern Territory, Australia may be over 50,000 years old.

▶ *The most famous cave paintings are those in the Hall of Bulls at Lascaux in France. These paintings show bison.*

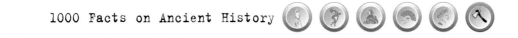

The Stone Ages

- **The Stone Ages** were the periods of time before humans discovered metals and so used mainly stones for making tools.

- **Stone tools** were made by chipping away stones to make hammers, spear heads and arrow heads, knives and scrapers.

- **People** usually used local stone, but sometimes good stones were imported from a long way away.

- **Early Europeans** used mainly flint for their stone tools. Africans used quartz, chert, basalt and obsidian.

- **In Europe**, there were three Stone Ages: Old (Palaeolithic), Middle (Mesolithic) and New (Neolithic).

- **The Palaeolithic** began 2 mya, when various human ancestors gathered plants and hunted with stone weapons.

- **The Mesolithic** was the transition from the Old to the New Stone Age – after the Last Ice Age ended around 12,000 years ago.

- **The Neolithic** was the time when people began to settle down and farm. This occurred first in the Near East, about 10,000 years ago.

◀ *A well-made, properly shaped stone tool could chop right through wood, meat, bone, and animal skin – even the toughest of hides.*

- **In 1981,** a pebble shaped into a female form, half a million years old was found at Berekhat Ram in Israel's Golan Heights.

- **Venus figurines** are plump stone female figures from *c.*25,000 years ago, found in Europe, e.g. the Czech Republic.

▶ *Mesolithic people hunted with bows and arrows and flint-tipped spears.*

21

The Bronze Age

- **The Bronze Age** is the period of prehistory when people first began to use the metal bronze.

- **Bronze is** an alloy (mix) of copper with about 10% tin.

- **The first metals** used were probably lumps of pure gold and copper, beaten into shape to make ornaments in Turkey and Iran about 6000BC.

- **Metal ores** (metals mixed with other minerals) were probably discovered when certain stones were found to melt when heated in a kiln.

- **Around 4000BC,** metalsmiths in southeast Europe and Iran began making copper axeheads with a central hole to take a wooden shaft.

- **The Copper Age** is the period when people used copper before they learned to alloy it with tin to make bronze. Metalworking with copper was flourishing in the early cities of Mesopotamia, in the Middle East, about 3500BC.

- **The Bronze Age** began several times between 3500 and 3000BC in the Near East, Balkans and Southeast Asia, when smiths discovered that, by adding a small quantity of tin, they could make bronze. Bronze is harder than copper and easier to make into a sharp blade.

▶ *A Bronze Age axe, 1500-700BC.*

● **Knowledge** of bronze spread slowly across Eurasia, but by 1500BC it was in use all the way from Europe to India.

● **The rarity** of tin spurred long-distance trade links – and the first mines, like the tin mines in Cornwall, England.

● **Bronze** can be cast – shaped by melting it into a clay mould (itself shaped with a wax model). For the first time people could make things any shape they wanted. Skilled smiths across Eurasia began to cast bronze to make everything from weapons to cooking utensils.

◀ *By 1000BC, beautiful metal swords and other weapons with sharp blades like this were being made all over Europe and western Asia.*

The Iron Age

- **The Iron Age** is the time in prehistory when iron replaced bronze as the main metal.

- **The use of iron** was discovered by the Hittites in Anatolia, Turkey between 1500 and 1200BC. This discovery helped to make the Hittites immensely powerful for a few centuries.

- **Around 1200BC,** the Hittite Empire collapsed and the use of iron spread through Asia and central Europe. The Dorian Greeks became famous iron masters.

- **Tin is rare,** so bronze objects were made mostly for chieftains. Iron ore is common, so ordinary people could have metal objects such as cooking utensils.

- **Many ordinary** farmers could afford iron scythes and axes. With tough metal tools to clear fields and harvest crops quickly, farming developed much more rapidly.

- **Growth in population** put pressure on resources and warfare increased across Eurasia. Partly as a result, many northern European settlements developed into hillforts – hilltop sites protected by earth ramparts, ditches and stockades.

- **Around 650BC,** peoples skilled in iron-working, called Celts, began to dominate northern Europe.

> ...**FASCINATING FACT**...
> In 1950, an Iron Age man was found in a peatbog at Tollund in Jutland, Denmark, perfectly preserved over 2000 years.

▶ *The easy availability of iron in the Iron Age meant that even a fairly poor man might have his own sword.*

24

- **Iron-working** reached China around 600BC. The Chinese used large bellows to boost furnace temperatures enough to melt iron ore in large quantities.

- **Iron tools** appearing in West Africa around 400BC were the basis of the Nok culture. Nok Farmers speaking Bantu languages spread south and east all over Africa.

Typical Iron Age round houses, built of wood and straw thatch

The hilltop village within the defences covered about 17 hectares

The inner rampart was 14 m high and topped by a fence of huge, upright timbers. It was faced with big limestone blocks, not grass

A series of ditches and banks were built up from clay

The approach to the entrance wound between ramparts to make life hard for attackers

The entrance through the inner ramparts had massive timber gates

▲ *Maiden Castle in Dorset is the largest of around 1000 hillforts built in southern Britain in the Iron Age. This is how it might have looked in about 300BC.*

25

Megaliths

- *Megalith* means 'giant stone'.

- **Megaliths are** monuments such as tombs made from huge blocks of stone, built in western Europe in the Neolithic and Bronze Ages between 4000 and 1500BC.

- **It was** once thought that megaliths began in one place. Now experts think they emerged in many areas.

- *Menhirs* are large standing stones. Sometimes they stand by themselves, sometimes in avenues or circles.

▼ *The most famous avenues of stone are at Carnac in Brittany, France, where thousands of stones stand in long lines.*

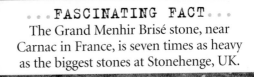

...**FASCINATING FACT**...
The Grand Menhir Brisé stone, near Carnac in France, is seven times as heavy as the biggest stones at Stonehenge, UK.

▶ *It took about 1,400 years to construct Stonehenge. The people of Stone Age Britain first built a ring of ditches, and giant stones from as far away as 350 km were slowly added. The biggest upright stones are 9 m high and weigh 50 tonnes. Stonehenge may have been a temple or astronomical observatory.*

- **The largest** known existing menhir is the Grand Menhir Brisé at Locmariaquer, near Carnac in France. This single stone once stood 20 m tall and weighed 280 tonnes.

- **The largest** stone circle is at Avebury in Wiltshire, southern England.

- **The most** famous stone circle is Stonehenge on Salisbury Plain, Wiltshire, built between 2950 and 1600BC.

- **Some megaliths** align with amazing accuracy with astronomical events, such as sunrise at the summer solstice (midsummer day) and may have acted as calendars.

- **Erecting** such stones took huge teams of men working with enormous wooden rollers, levers and ropes.

Archaeology

- **Archaeology** is the scientific study of relics left by humans in the past, from old bones to ancient temples.

- **Most archaeological** relics are buried beneath the ground or sunk beneath the sea.

- **Aerial** photographs often reveal where archaeologists should dig. Crops and grass will grow differently if the soil is affected by a buried wall or filled-in ditch.

▲ *Archaeological digging is a very painstaking process. Diggers work with immense care to avoid overlooking or breaking tiny, fragile relics.*

- **Geophysical** surveys involve using metal detectors and other electronic probes to pick up features underground.

- **Field walking** involves walking over the site, carefully scanning the ground by eye for tiny relics.

- **During a dig,** archaeologists dig carefully down through the layers. They note exactly where every relic was found, in case its position helps to reveal the story behind the site.

pottery   statue   lamps   jewellery

Archaeologists have found many remains of Roman life. Roman pottery was beautifully made and designed, while statues give an idea of how Romans looked. Oil-burning lamps have been unearthed, and we know that the Romans loved beautiful jewellery.

- **Archaeologists** call on many different kinds of expert to help them to interpret finds. Forensic scientists may help to tell how a skeleton died, for instance.

- **The deeper** a relic is buried, the older it is likely to be.

- **Radio carbon** dating is a way of dating the remains of once-living things from their carbon content. This is accurate up to 50,000 years ago.

- **Potassium** argon dating helps to date the rocks in which relics were found from their potassium and argon content. Human remains in Africa were dated in this way.

▶ An archaelogist's dig uncovers remains from the Roman period. We can gain greater understanding of Roman life from the evidence unearthed.

29

The first farms

- **Starch marks** on stone implements found in Papua New Guinea suggest yams may have been grown there at least 30,000 years ago.

- **Water chestnuts** and beans may have been farmed near Spirit Cave in north Vietnam from 11,000 to 7500BC.

- **About 9000BC,** some people abandoned the old way of life, hunting animals and gathering fruit, and settled down to farm. Experts call this great change the Neolithic Revolution.

- **Farming began** as people planted grasses for their seed (or grain) in the Near East, in Guangdong in China and in Latin America – and perhaps planted root vegetables in Peru and Indonesia, too.

- **Emmer wheat** and barley were grown in the Near East *c.*8000BC. Sheep and goats were tamed here soon after.

- **The ox-drawn** plough was used from *c.*5000BC. The Chinese used hand ploughs even earlier.

- **Crop irrigation** canals were dug at Choya Mami, near Mandali in Iraq, between 5500 and 4750BC.

- **China, the Indus,** Egypt and Babylonia all had extensive irrigation systems in place by 3000BC.

- **The first farmers** reaped their grain with sickles of flint.

- **Farmers** soon learned to store food. Underground granaries at Ban-Po, Shansi, China, date from *c.*4800BC.

▲ *Farming began about 11,000 years ago, as people began saving grass seed to grow so that they could grind new seed into flour.*

The first cities

- **The walls** of the city of Jericho on the river Jordan, in the Near East, are 11,000 years old, and the city has been continuously occupied longer than anywhere else in the world.

- **People** began to live in towns when farming produced enough extra food for people to specialize in crafts such as basket-making and for people to begin to trade with each other.

- **Villages** and towns probably first developed in the Near East in the Neolithic period, about 8000BC.

- *Tells* **are** mounds that have built up at ancient settlement sites (in the Near and Middle East) from mud-brick houses that have crumbled.

- **The most** famous ancient town is Catal Hüyük in Anatolia, in Turkey, which was occupied from 7000 to 5500BC. 10,000 people may have lived here.

- **The houses** in Catal Hüyük were made from mud bricks covered with fine plaster. Some rooms were shrines, with bulls' heads and mother goddesses.

- **Asikli Hüyük** is a nearby forerunner of Catal Hüyük, dating from over a thousand years earlier.

- **The first big** city was Eridu in Mesopotamia (modern Iraq's Abu Shahrain Tell) which has a temple dating from 4900BC.

- **50,000 people** were living in Sumerian Uruk (modern Warka) on the banks of the Euphrates River in Iraq in 3500BC.

- **Sumerian Ur** was the first city to have a population of a quarter of a million, by about 2500BC.

▲ *Houses in Catal Hüyük were so tightly packed that people had to walk over flat roofs to get to their home, and then climb down a ladder to enter through an opening.*

33

'Between rivers'

- **Mesopotamia** lies between the Tigris and Euphrates rivers in Turkey, Syria and Iraq. *Mesopotamia* is Greek for 'between rivers'.

- **Mesopotamia** is called the 'cradle of civilization' because many ancient civilizations arose here, including the Sumerian, Babylonian and Assyrian.

- **The first great** civilization was that of the Sumerians, who farmed irrigated land by the Euphrates *c.*5000BC and lived in mud-brick houses.

- **By 4000BC,** the settlements of Eridu, Uruk and Ur had grown into towns with water supplies and drainage systems, as well as palaces and mountain-shaped temple-mounds called *ziggurats*.

- **Sumerians** devised the first writing system (cuneiform), made with wedge-shaped marks on clay tablets.

▲ *By 3200BC, carts like this were being used in Sumer. No one knows when the wheel was invented. It probably developed from potters' wheels.*

- **Sumerians** cast all kinds of beautiful objects – first from copper, then, from 3500BC, in bronze.

- **The Sumerian** *Epic of Gilgamesh* tells of a flood similar to that in the biblical story of Noah's Ark.

- **The Sumerians** developed the first known elaborate systems of law and government.

- **At first, each** city or 'city-state' was run by a council of elders, but in wartime a *lugal* (leader) took charge. By 2900BC, the lugals had become kings and ruled all the time.

- **In 2350BC,** Sumer was overrun by Sargon of Akkad, but Sumerian power was re-established at Ur in 2150BC.

▶ *The* Epic of Gilgamesh *was composed around 2000BC. It tells the tale of Gilgamesh (right), a powerful and oppressive king in ancient Sumeria. When his people pray for help, the gods create Enkidu, who meets Gilgamesh in battle. But the two become friends and share many adventures. The poem concludes with a great flood, which has been likened to the Bible story of Noah.*

Indus civilization

- **About 3000**BC, a civilization developed from small farming communities in the Indus valley in Pakistan.

- **The remains** of over 100 towns of the Indus civilization have been found. The main sites are Mohenjo-Daro, Harappa, Kalibangan and Lothal.

- **Indus cities** were carefully planned, with straight streets, bath-houses and big granaries (grain stores).

- **At the centre** was a fortified citadel, built on a platform of bricks. The rulers probably lived here.

- **Indus houses** were built of brick around a central courtyard. They had several rooms, a toilet and a well.

- **The Indus** civilization had its own system of writing, which appears on objects such as carved seals – but no one has yet been able to decipher it.

- **Single-room huts** at all intersections are thought to be police-posts.

- **Mohenjo-Daro** and Harappa had 35,000 inhabitants each by about 2500BC.

▼ *Seals like this were used by Indus merchants to stamp bales of goods.*

● **By 1750BC**, the Indus civilization had declined, perhaps because floods changed the course of the Indus River. War may also have played a part. It finally vanished with the arrival of the Aryans in India about 1500BC.

▲ *The people of Mohenjo-Daro used ox-drawn carts. However, this form of transport would have been very slow and they probably relied on the river as their main source of transportation.*

. . . **FASCINATING FACT** . . .
Soapstone trading seals from the Indus
civilization have been found as far away
as Bahrain and Ur.

Great migrations

- **The first migrations** occurred when human-like *Homo ergaster* walked out of Africa 750,000 years ago.

- **Experts** once thought that oceans had blocked migrations but it now seems that boats have been used since the earliest days.

- **100,000 years ago,** humans moved out of Africa into the Near East.

- **About 50,000 years ago,** humans began the great expansion that took them to every continent but Antarctica within 20,000 years – and replaced Neanderthal Man.

- **50,000-40,000 years ago,** humans spread across Asia and Australasia. 40,000-35,000 ya, they moved into Europe. 30,000-25,000 years ago, they trekked out of northeast Asia and crossed into the Americas.

- **Early humans** were mainly nomadic hunters, always on the move, following animals into empty lands.

- **Changes in** climate triggered many migrations. People moved north in warm times and retreated in Ice Ages. When the last Ice Age ended, 10,000 years ago, hunters moved north through Europe as the weather warmed. Those left behind in the Middle East settled down to farm.

▶ *Just like American pioneers in the 1800s, Aryans living 4000 years ago moved their families and possessions in covered wagons, probably pulled by oxen.*

▲ *During the Ice Age people used spears made from bone, antler or flint to bring down animals such as huge, woolly mammoths.*

- **From 9000 to 7000 years ago**, farming spread northwest across Europe – partly through people actually moving, partly by word of mouth.

- **4000 years ago**, Indo-Europeans spread out from their home in southern Russia. They went south into Iran (as Mittanians) and India (Aryans), south-west into Turkey (Hittites) and Greece (Mycenaeans) and into the west (Celts).

- **About 3000 years ago**, the Sahara area began to dry up, and people living there moved to the fringes. Bantu-speaking people from Nigeria and the Congo spread south through Africa.

39

Ancient Egypt

- **While dozens** of cities were developing in Mesopotamia, in Egypt the foundations were being laid for the first great nation.

- **From 5000-3300BC**, farmers by the river Nile banded together to dig canals to control the Nile's annual flooding and to water their crops.

- **By 3300BC**, Nile farming villages had grown into towns. Rich and powerful kings were buried in big, box-like mud-brick tombs called *mastabas*.

- **Egyptian** townspeople began to work copper and stone, paint vases, weave baskets and use potters' wheels.

- **Early Egypt** was divided into two kingdoms: Upper Egypt, and Lower Egypt on the Nile delta. In 3100BC, King Menes of Upper Egypt conquered Lower Egypt to unite the two kingdoms, but a king of Egypt was always called King of Upper and Lower Egypt.

▶ *The ancient Egyptians built great cities and monuments along the Nile valley during the days of the Old Kingdom.*

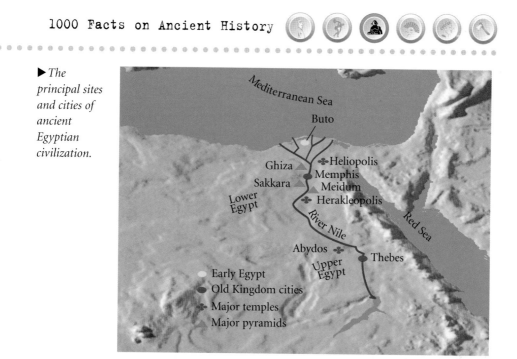

▶ *The principal sites and cities of ancient Egyptian civilization.*

Mediterranean Sea

Buto

Ghiza
Heliopolis
Memphis
Sakkara
Meidum
Lower
Egypt
Herakleopolis

River Nile

Red Sea

Abydos
Upper
Egypt
Thebes

○ Early Egypt
● Old Kingdom cities
✿ Major temples
▲ Major pyramids

- **Menes founded** a capital for united Egypt at Memphis.

- **With Menes,** Egypt's Dynasty I – the first family of kings – began. The time of Dynasties I and II, which lasted until 2649BC, is known by historians as the Archaic Period.

- **After the** Archaic Period came the Old Kingdom (2649-2134BC), perhaps the greatest era of Egyptian culture.

- **Craftsmen** made fine things, scholars developed writing and the calendar and studied astronomy and maths.

- **The greatest** scholar and priest was Imhotep, minister to King Zoser (2630-2611BC). Imhotep was architect of the first of the great pyramids, the Step Pyramid at Sakkara.

Babylon

- **Babylon** was one of the greatest cities of the ancient world. It stood on the banks of the Euphrates River, near what is now Al Hillah in Iraq.

- **Babylon** reached its peak in two phases: the Old Babylonian Empire (1792-1234BC) and the New Babylonian Empire (626-539BC).

- **Babylon** first grew as a city from 2200BC, but only when Hammurabi became king in 1792BC did it become powerful. In his 42-year reign, Hammurabi's conquests gave Babylon a huge empire in Mesopotamia.

- **Hammurabi** was a great law-maker, and some of his laws were enscribed on a stone pillar, or stele, now in the Louvre in Paris. One of his main laws was that 'the strong shall not oppress the weak'. There were also laws to punish crimes and protect people from poor workmanship by builders and doctors.

▼ *The Greeks described the Hanging Gardens of Babylon as one of the Seven Wonders of the ancient world. Nebuchadnezzar II is said to have had them built for his wife, who missed the greenery of her mountain home.*

Gardens of lush trees and flowers filled rising brick terraces

The gardens were on a huge pyramid of brick and tar, 25 m high

Water for the plants was continually raised from the river by screw pumps wound by slaves

- **After Hammurabi** died, Babylonian power declined and the Assyrians gained the upper hand. After long Babylonian resistance, the Assyrians destroyed the city in 689BC, only to rebuild it 11 years later.

- **Just 60 years** or so later, Babylonian king Nabopolassar and his son Nebuchadnezzar II crushed the Assyrians and built the new Babylonian Empire.

- **Under Nebuchadnezzar II,** Babylon became a vast, magnificent city of 250,000 people, with grand palaces, temples and houses.

▲ *Under Nebuchadnezzar II (630-562BC), Babylon achieved its greatest fame. He is known for conquering Jerusalem and for his great building projects.*

- **Babylon** was surrounded by walls 26 m thick – glazed with blue bricks, decorated with dragons, lions and bulls and pierced by eight huge bronze gates. The grandest gate was the Ishtar Gate, which opened on to a paved avenue called the Processional Street.

- **Babylonians** were so sure of their power that King Belshazzar was having a party when the Persians, led by Cyrus, attacked. Cyrus's men dug canals to divert the Euphrates River, then slipped into the city along the riverbed. Cyrus wrote on the walls for Belshazzar, 'You are weighed in the balance, and are found wanting.'

> **FASCINATING FACT**
> Dying of a fever, Macedonian king Alexander the Great found cool relief in Babylon's Hanging Gardens.

Early China

- **In China**, farming communities known as the Yanshao culture developed by the Huang He (Yellow River) 7000 years ago. By 5000BC, the region was ruled by emperors.

- **Early Chinese** emperors are known of only by legend. Huang-Ti, the Yellow Emperor, was said to have become emperor in 2697BC.

- **In about 2690BC,** Huang-Ti's wife, Hsi-Ling Shi, discovered how to use the cocoon of the silkworm (the caterpillar of the *Bombyx mori* moth) to make silk. Hsi-Ling was afterwards known as Seine-Than (the Silk Goddess).

- **By 2000BC,** the Chinese were making beautiful jade carvings.

- **The Hsias family** were said to be one of the earliest dynasties of Chinese emperors, ruling from 2000 to 1750BC.

◀ *The Shang emperors were warriors. Their soldiers fought in padded bamboo armour.*

- **The Shangs** were the first definitely known dynasty of emperors. They came to power in 1750BC.

- **Shang emperors** had their fortune told every few days from cracks on heated animal bones. Marks on these 'oracle' bones are the oldest examples of Chinese writing.

- **Under the** Shangs, the Chinese became skilled bronze-casters.

- **In the Shang** cities of Anyang and Zengzhou, thick-walled palace temples were surrounded at a distance by villages of artisans.

- **Shang emperors** went to their tombs along with their servants and captives, as well as entire chariots with their horses and drivers.

▲ *Silkworms (the larvae, or young, of the* Bombyx mori *moth) feed on mulberry leaves. Silk was invented in China, and for many years the method of making it was kept a closely guarded secret.*

45

Egyptian writing

- **Ancient Egyptian** writing developed between 3300 and 3100BC – perhaps inspired by Sumerian scripts.

- **Egyptian writing** is called *hieroglyphic* (Greek for 'holy writing'). The Egyptians called it the 'words of the gods', because they believed writing was given by the god Thoth.

- **The last known** hieroglyphs were written in AD394, long after anyone knew how to read them.

- **In AD1799,** the French soldiers of Napoleon's army found a stone slab at Rosetta in Egypt. It was covered in three identical texts

- **In AD1822,** Jean-François Champollion deciphered the Rosetta stone, realizing that hieroglyphs are pictures that stand for sounds and letters, and not just for objects.

- **There were** 700 hieroglyphsin common use. Most are pictures and can be written from left to right, right to left or downwards.

▲ *When Frenchman Jean-François Champollion translated the Greek text on the Rosetta stone, he was able to crack the code to its passage of hieroglyphs.*

▲ *The walls of Egyptian tombs are covered in hieroglyphs.*

- **Words inside** an oval shape called a *cartouche* are the names of pharaohs.

- **There were** two shorthand versions of hieroglyphs for everyday use – early hieratic script and later demotic script.

- **Egyptians** not only wrote on tomb walls but wrote everyday things with ink and brushes on papyrus (paper made from papyrus reeds) or on *ostraca* (pottery fragments).

- **Only highly** trained scribes could write. Scribes were very well paid and often exempt from taxes.

▲ *Papyrus was made by taking wet strips of the pithy stems of papyrus plants and pressing them side by side.*

47

Egyptian life

- **Egyptians** washed every day in the river or with a jug and basin. The rich were given showers by servants.

- **Instead of** soap they used a cleansing cream made from oil, lime and perfume. They also rubbed themselves all over with moisturizing oil.

- **Egyptian** women painted their nails with henna and reddened their lips and cheeks with red ochre paste.

- **Egyptian** fashions changed little over thousands of years, and their clothes were usually white linen.

- **Men wrapped** linen round themselves in a kilt. Women wore long, light dresses. Children ran around naked during the summer.

▲ *Egyptian women were highly conscious of their looks, wearing make-up and jewellery and dressing their hair with great care.*

- **Every Egyptian** wore jewellery. The rich wore gold inlaid with gems; the poor wore copper or faience (made by heating powdered quartz).

- **Egyptians** loved to play board games. Their favourites were 'senet' and 'hounds and jackals'.

- **Rich Egyptians** held lavish parties with food and drink, singers, musicians, acrobats and dancing girls.

- **Rich Egyptians** often went fishing or boating.

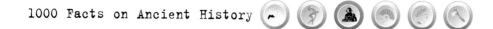
▶ *In ancient Egypt, a man provided for his family, and his wife ran the home and was held in great respect. Some couples lived with the parents of the husband or wife.*

....FASCINATING FACT...
Egyptian men and women wore kohl
eyeliner, made from the minerals
malachite and galena.

Ancient Crete

- **The Minoan** civilization of Crete – an island south of Greece – was the first civilization in Europe.

- **Minoan** civilization began about 3000BC, reached its height from 2200 to 1450BC, then mysteriously vanished – perhaps after the volcano on nearby Santorini erupted.

- **The name** *Minoan* comes from the Greek legend of King Minos. Minos was the son of Europa, the princess seduced by the god Zeus in the shape of a bull.

- **Greek stories** tell how Minos built a labyrinth (maze) in which he kept the Minotaur, a monster with a man's body and a bull's head.

- **Catching a bull** by the horns and leaping over it (bull-leaping) was an important Minoan religious rite.

- **Experts** now think Minos was a title, so every Cretan king was called Minos.

- **The Minoans** were great seafarers and traded all over the eastern Mediterranean.

- **At the centre** of each Minoan town was a palace, such as those found at Knossos, Zakro, Phaestos and Mallia.

▲ *The minotaur of Greek myth.*

50

- **The largest** Minoan palace is at Knossos. It covered 20,000 square metres and housed over 30,000 people.

- **The walls** of the palace are decorated with frescoes (paintings), which reveal a great deal about the Minoans.

▼ *The famous Minoan palace at Knossos*

The pharaohs

- **Pharaohs** were the kings of Ancient Egypt. They were also High Priest, head judge and commander of the army.

- **Egyptians** thought of the pharaoh as both the god Horus and the son of the sun god Re. When he died he was transformed into the god Osiris, father of Horus. Since he was a god, anyone approaching him had to crawl.

- **The pharaoh** was thought to be so holy that he could not be addressed directly. Instead, people referred to him indirectly by talking of the pharaoh, which is Egyptian for 'great house'. Only after about 945BC was he addressed directly as the pharaoh.

- **In official** documents the pharaoh had five titles: Horus; Two Ladies; Golden Horus; King of Upper and Lower Egypt and Lord of the Double Land (Upper and Lower Egypt); and Son of Re and Lord of the Diadems.

- **The pharaoh's** godlike status gave him magical powers. His *uraeus* (the snake on his crown) was supposed to spit flames at his enemies and the pharaoh was said to be able to trample thousands.

- **There were** 31 dynasties (families) of pharaohs, beginning with Menes in c.3100BC and ending with the Persian kings in 323BC. Each dynasty is identified in order by a Roman numeral. So the fifth dynasty is Dynasty V.

- **A pharaoh** usually married his eldest sister to keep the royal blood pure. She became queen and was known as the Royal Heiress, but the pharaoh had many other wives. If the pharaoh died while his eldest son was still a child, his queen became regent and ruled on his behalf.

> ...**FASCINATING FACT**...
> People thought the pharaoh had the power to control the weather and to make the land fertile.

- **To preserve** their bodies forever, pharaohs were buried inside massive tombs. The first pharaohs were buried in huge pyramids. Because these were often robbed, later pharaohs were buried in tombs cut deep into cliffs.

- **One of the** greatest pharaohs was Ramses II, who ruled from 1290 to 1224BC. He left a legacy of many huge buildings, including the rock temple of Abu Simbel.

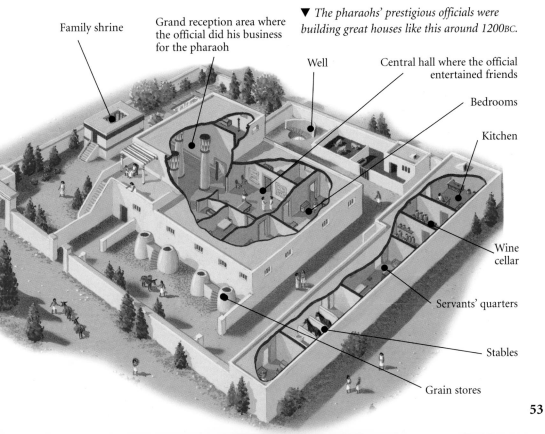

▼ *The pharaohs' prestigious officials were building great houses like this around 1200BC.*

Family shrine

Grand reception area where the official did his business for the pharaoh

Well

Central hall where the official entertained friends

Bedrooms

Kitchen

Wine cellar

Servants' quarters

Stables

Grain stores

Olmecs and Chavins

- **People began** farming in Meso America (Mexico and Central America) 9000 years ago, almost as long ago as in the Middle East.

- **By 2000BC**, there were permanent villages and large farms growing corn, beans, squash and other crops.

- **Between 1200** and 400BC, a remarkable culture was developed by the Olmecs in western Mexico.

- **The Olmecs** had a counting system and calendar, but no writing system, so little is known about them.

- **Ruins of a huge** Olmec pyramid have been found at La Venta in Tabasco, Mexico.

▲ *The Olmec heads were carved from huge blocks of volcanic rock weighing up to 14 tonnes. No one knows how they were moved.*

- **The Olmecs** carved huge 'baby-face' heads from basalt with enormous skill – apparently with only stone chisels, since they had no metal.

- **By 2000BC,** huge religious sites were being built all over what is now Peru, in South America.

- **From 800** to 400BC, the Chavin civilization spread from the religious centre of Chavin de Huantar in the Peruvian mountains.

- **From AD100** to 700, America's first true city developed at Teotihuacán, with vast pyramids and palaces.
- **Teotihuacán** may have been the world's biggest city in AD300, with a population of over 250,000.

▼ *The ruins of Teotihuacán.*

Aryan India

- **The Aryans** were a lighter-skinned herding people from southern Russia, ancestors to both Greeks and Indians.

- **About 2000BC,** the Aryan people began to sweep through Persia and on into India, where they destroyed the Indus civilizations.

- **The Aryans** were tough warriors who loved music, dancing and chariot racing, but slowly adopted Dravidian gods and settled in villages as farmers.

▲ *The dark-skinned Dravidian people who were living in India when the Aryans arrived became the servant class.*

- **Aryan people** were originally split into three categories: *Brahmins* (priests) at the top, *Kshatriya* (warriors) in the middle and *Vaisyas* (merchants and farmers) at the bottom.

- **When they** settled in India, the Aryans added a fourth category – the conquered, dark-skinned Dravidians, who became their servants.

- **From the** four Aryan classes, the elaborate system of castes (classes) in today's India developed.

- **The Aryans** gave India the language of Sanskrit.

- **Ancient Sanskrit** is closely related to European languages such as Latin, English and German.

- **The Aryans** had no form of writing, but they passed on history and religion by word of mouth in spoken *Books of Knowledge*, or *Vedas*.

- **The Brahmins** created the first Hindu scriptures as *Vedas*, including the *Rig-Veda*, the *Sama-Veda* and *Yajur-Veda*.

धेनुः ग्राम्यः पशुः ।

▲ *Sanskrit is the oldest literary language of India, and simply translated it means 'refined' or 'polished'. It forms the basis of many modern Indian languages such as Hindi and Urdu – the national language of Pakistan.*

Semites

- **Jewish people** and Arabs are Semitic people.

- **In 2500BC,** the Semites were farming peoples such as the Akkadians, Canaanites and Amorites, who lived in what is now Israel, Jordan and Syria.

- **In 2371BC,** an Akkadian called Sargon seized the throne of the Sumerian city of Kish. He conquered all Sumer and Akkad and created a great empire.

- **The Akkadian** Empire collapsed c.2230BC, under attacks from tribes of Gutians from the mountains.

- **From 3000** to 1500BC, Canaanite Byblos was one of the world's great trading ports, famous for its purple cloth.

- **c.2000BC,** Amorites conquered Sumer, Akkad and Canaan. In 1792BC, the Amorite Hammurabi was ruler of Babylon.

- **The first** Hebrews were a Semitic tribe from southern Mesopotamia. Their name meant 'people of the other side' – of the Euphrates River.

- **According** to the Bible, the first Hebrew was Abraham, a shepherd who lived in the Sumerian city of Ur, 4000 years ago. He led his family first to Syria, then to Canaan (now Palestine), where he settled.

- **Abraham's** grandson Jacob was also called Israel and the Hebrews were afterwards called Israelites.

- **About 1000BC,** the Israelite people prospered under three kings – Saul, David and Solomon.

▶ *The* Dead Sea Scrolls *are ancient Hebrew manuscripts found by shepherds in 1947 in a cave near the Dead Sea. They include the oldest known texts of the Bible's Old Testament. Today the Scrolls are housed in a museum in Israel.*

The Assyrians

- **The Assyrians** came originally from the upper Tigris valley around the cities of Ashur, Nineveh and Arbela.

- *c.*2000BC, Assyria was invaded by Amorites. Under a line of Amorite kings, Assyria built up a huge empire. King Adadnirari I called himself 'King of Everything'.

- **The Old** Assyrian Empire lasted six centuries, until it was broken by attacks by Mitannian horsemen.

- **From 1114** to 1076BC, King Tiglath Pileser I rebuilt Assyrian power by conquest, creating the New Assyrian Empire.

> ...**FASCINATING FACT**...
> King Assurbanipal's (668-627BC) palace was filled with books and plants from all over the world.

◀ *Assyrian stone carvings were skillfully done. Many, such as this one showing a genie, decorated palace walls.*

60

- **The New** Assyrian Empire reached its peak under Tiglath-Pileser III (744-727BC) and was finally overthrown by the Medes and Babylonians in 612BC.

- **The Assyrians** were ruthless warriors. They grew beards and fought with bows, iron swords, spears and chariots.

- **The Assyrians** built good roads all over their empire, so that the army could move fast to quell trouble.

- **The Assyrians** built magnificent palaces and cities such as Khorsabad and Nimrud.

- **Arab warriors** rode camels into battle for the Assyrians.

▶ *Wealthy Assyrians strove to outdo each other with elaborate clothing and luxurious houses.*

Oceania

- **The people** of the Pacific – Oceania – may have been the greatest seafarers of the ancient world.

- **Up until** 5000 years ago, the sea level was lower and Tasmania, Australia and New Guinea were all part of one big continent.

- **About** 50,000 years ago, bold, seafaring people crossed the ocean from Southeast Asia and settled in Australia.

- **Most early** sites are now lost offshore under the sea, which rose to cut off New Guinea and Australia c.5000BC.

- **The Australian** aboriginals are descendants of these original inhabitants.

- **The oldest** settlement in New Guinea is 40,000 years old.

- **c.4000BC,** domesticated plants and animals reached New Guinea from Asia, and farmers drained fields around an area called Kuk Swamp. Many people, however, remained hunters.

- **About 2000BC,** people sailed in canoes from Indonesia to colonize Melanesia and Micronesia – the islands of the western Pacific, such as Vanuatu.

- **Early Melanesians** are known by their 'Lapita' pottery, which originated in the Molucca Islands of Indonesia.

- **Rowing** canoes shown in a 50,000-year-old cave painting in Australia match those that can be seen all over the Pacific, and in caves in South America's Amazon jungle.

▶ *The people of Oceania crossed the oceans in canoes like these tens of thousands of years before the great European explorers.*

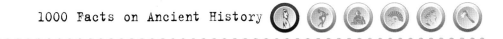

The afterlife

- **Egyptians** saw death as a step on the way to a fuller life in the Next World.

- **Everyone** was thought to have three souls: the *ka*, *ba* and *akh*. For these to flourish, the body must survive intact, so the ancient Egyptians tried to preserve their dead bodies as well as they could.

- **Gradually,** the Egyptians developed embalming techniques to preserve the bodies of kings and rich people who could afford it.

- **The organs** were cut out and stored in *canopic* jars and the body was dried with *natron* (a naturally occurring compound of salts).

- **The dried** body was filled with sawdust, resin and natron, then wrapped in bandages. The embalmed body is called a 'mummy'.

- **A portrait** mask was put over the mummy's head, and it was then put into a coffin.

- **Anthropoid** (human-shaped) coffins were used from about 2000BC onwards. Often, the mummy was put inside a nest of two or three coffins, each carved and painted and perhaps decorated with gold and gems.

- **The wooden** coffin was laid inside a stone coffin or sarcophagus inside the burial chamber.

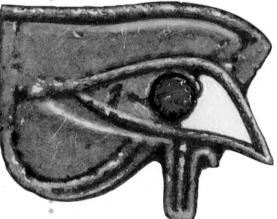

▲ *Egyptians carried amulets (charms), to ward off bad spirits. This one shows the eye of the all-powerful Egyptian god, Horus.*

- **At first,** the prayers said for a dead ruler were carved on pyramid walls as 'Pyramid Texts'. Later, they were put on coffins as 'Coffin Texts'. From 1500BC, they were written on papyrus in the *Book of the Dead*.

- **To help** him overcome various tests and make it to the Next World, a dead man needed amulets and a *Book of the Dead*, containing magic spells and a map.

▼ *When placing the mask over a mummy, the chief embalmer himself wore a mask, representing the jackal god, Anubis.*

Persia

- **Iran** is named after the Aryan people who began settling there *c.*15,000BC. Two Aryan tribes – the Medes and Persians – soon became dominant.

- **In 670BC,** the Medes under King Cyaxeres joined forces with the Babylonians and finally overthrew the Assyrians.

- **In 550BC,** the Medes themselves were overthrown by the Persians. The Persian king, Cyrus II, was the grandson of the king of the Medes, Astyages.

▼ Darius the Great ruled Persia from 521 until 486BC.

- **Cyrus II** had an army of horsemen and very skilled archers. He went on to establish a great Persian empire after conquering Lydia and Babylon.

- **The Persian** Empire was ruled by the Achaemenid family until it was destroyed by Alexander the Great in 330BC.

- **The Persian** Empire reached its greatest extent under Darius I, who called himself Shahanshah ('King of kings'). Darius introduced gold and silver coins, and also brought chickens to the Middle East.

- **Darius** built a famous road system and split his empire into 20 *satrapies* (regions), each ruled by a *satrap*.

- **'King's Ears'** were officials who travelled around the empire and reported any trouble back to the king.

- **The Persians** built luxurious cities and palaces – first at Susa, then in Darius's reign, at Persepolis.

● **Persian priests,** or *magi*, were known for their magic skills, and gave us the word 'magic'. A famous magus called Zarathustra, unusually, worshipped a single god: Ahuru Mazda. His god's evil enemy was Angra Mainyu.

◀ *Rich carvings adorned the walls at Persepolis – the great city and palace of Darius's reign.*

Weapons of war

● **Early** stone axes and spears may have been used both for hunting and as weapons. Remains of a wooden spear from half a million years ago were found at Boxgrove, England.

● **A spear-thrower** was a stick with a notch in one end to take the end of a spear. With it, hunters (or fighters) could hurl a spear with tremendous force. Spear-throwers were the first ever machines made by humans, *c.*35,000BC.

● **The first** pictures of bows come from North Africa, *c.*30,000-15,000BC. Bows could be devastatingly effective and were the main weapons of the earliest civilizations.

● **The invention** of bronze, *c.*3000BC, meant that people could make metal swords, daggers, axes and spears.

● **A tiny** bronze statue of a chariot found at Tell Agrab, Iraq, dates from 3000BC. This is the first image of a chariot.

◀ *Legendary warrior Alexander the Great, king of Macedonia, led vast numbers of soldiers who used artillery crossbows to fire huge arrows.*

- **The Persian** emperor Cyrus (559-529BC) added scythes (long, sharp blades) poking out sideways from chariot wheels to slice through the legs of enemy soldiers and horses.

- **The oldest** helmet (*c.*2500BC), made of a gold and silver alloy (mix) called electrum, was found in the royal tombs of Ur.

- **The crossbow** was invented in the Greek colony of Syracuse, about 400BC.

- **Alexander** the Great used crossbows, firing 5-m arrows, to win his empire between 340 and 323BC.

- **Around AD100,** Dionysius of Alexander in Egypt invented a rapid-firing crossbow, able to fire dozens of bolts a minute.

▼ *The chariot was the air force of the ancient civilizations, carrying archers and spear-throwers across the battlefield. Egyptians, Hittites and Assyrians fought huge battles with thousands of chariots.*

69

Tutankhamun

- **Tutankhamun** was pharaoh (king) of ancient Egypt from 1347 to 1339BC. He was a boy when he became pharaoh and only 18 when he died.

- **Tutankhamun** was the last of the great 18th dynasty (family) of pharaohs who ruled Egypt 1567-1339BC. They included the warrior queen Hatshepsut, and Thutmose III, who led Egypt to the peak of its power, around 1400BC.

- **Tutankhamun** was the son of Akhenaten, who with his queen Nefertiti created a revolution in Egypt. Akhenaten replaced worship of the old Egyptian gods with worship of a single god, and moved the capital to Armarna.

- **Tutankhamun's** wife was his half-sister Ankhesenamun. When he died – perhaps murdered – Ankhesenamun was at the mercy of his enemies, Ay and General Horemheb. She wrote to the Hittite king asking for his son to marry, but the Hittite prince was murdered on the way to Egypt. Ankhesenamun was forced to marry Ay, who thus became pharaoh. She also died young.

- **The Valley** of the Kings, near Luxor on the river Nile in Egypt, is the world's greatest archaeological site. It was the special burial place of the 18th dynasty pharaohs and contains the tombs of 62 pharaohs, and high officials.

▲ *A fabulous gold mask was found in Tutankhamun's innermost coffin, over the young king's decaying remains. His skull showed signs of hammer blows.*

> ....FASCINATING FACT....
> Tutankhamun's third, inner coffin was
> made of over a tonne of solid gold.

- **Tutankhamun's** tomb was the only tomb in the Valley of the Kings not plundered over the centuries. When opened, it contained 5000 items, including many fabulous carved and gold items.

- **Tutankhamun's** tomb was discovered by the English archaeologist Howard Carter, in 1922.

- **Rumours** of a curse on those disturbing the tomb began when Carter's pet canary was eaten by a cobra – the symbol of the pharaoh – at the moment the tomb was first opened.

- **Experts** worked out the dates of Tutankhamun's reign from the date labels on wine-jars left in the tomb.

▼ *When Carter opened Tutankhamun's tomb, he came first to an anteroom. It took him three years to clear this room and enter the burial chamber, with its huge gold shrines containing the coffins.*

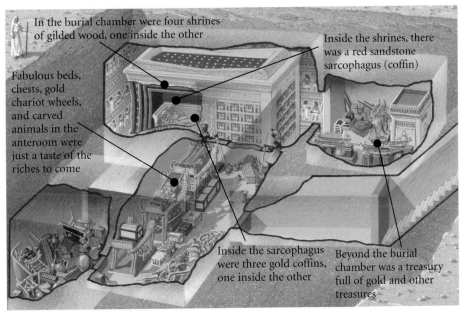

In the burial chamber were four shrines of gilded wood, one inside the other

Inside the shrines, there was a red sandstone sarcophagus (coffin)

Fabulous beds, chests, gold chariot wheels, and carved animals in the anteroom were just a taste of the riches to come

Inside the sarcophagus were three gold coffins, one inside the other

Beyond the burial chamber was a treasury full of gold and other treasures

71

The Trojan Wars

- **From 1600** to 1100BC, mainland Greece was dominated by tough warrior people called the Mycenaeans.

- **The Mycenaeans** fought with long bronze swords, long leather shields and bronze armour.

- **Mycenaeans** lived in small kingdoms, each with its own fortified hilltop city – called an *acropolis*.

- **A typical** Mycenaean noble was like a Viking chieftain. In the middle of his palace was a great hall with a central fireplace where warriors would sit around, telling tales of heroic deeds.

- **After 1500BC**, Mycenaean kings were buried in a beehive-shaped tomb called a *tholos*, with a long, corridor-shaped entrance.

- **The Greek** poet Homer tells how a city called Troy was destroyed by the Mycenaeans after a ten-year siege. Historians once thought this was just a story, but now that Troy's remains have been discovered, they think there may be some truth in it.

▶ *Troy fell when the Greeks pretended to give up and go home, leaving behind a huge wooden horse. The jubilant Trojans dragged this into the city – only to discover Greeks hiding inside it.*

▶ *The Trojan War lasted for ten bloody years. Many lives were lost during battles, even though the soldiers wore protective armour. Achilles and Hector would have worn crested helmets like those shown here, to make them look more frightening and impressive. A bronze breast plate would have protected the upper body while bronze leg guards were worn to protect the lower legs.*

- **The Trojan** War in Homer's tale is caused by the beautiful Helen of Sparta. She married Menalaus, brother of King Agamemnon of Mycenae, but she fell in love with Prince Paris of Troy.

- **Helen and Paris** eloped to Troy and Agamemnon and other Greeks laid siege to Troy to take her back.

- **The battle** featured many heroes – such as Hector, Achilles and Odysseus.

- **The Greeks** finally captured Troy when Greek soldiers hidden inside a wooden horse found their way into the city.

Early Greece

- **Around 1200BC,** the Mycenaeans began to abandon their cities, and a people called the Dorians took over Greece.

- **Many Mycenaeans** fled overseas in a large battle fleet, and the Egyptians called them the Sea Peoples. Some ended up in Italy and may have been the ancestors of the Etruscan people there.

- **With the end** of Mycenaean civilization, Greece entered its Dark Ages as the art of writing was lost.

- **About 800BC,** the Greeks began to emerge from their Dark Ages as they relearned writing from the Phoenicians, a people who traded in the eastern Mediterranean.

- **The period** of Greek history from 800 to 500BC is called the Archaic (Ancient) Period.

- **In the Archaic** Period, the Greek population grew rapidly. States were governed by rich aristocrats.

◄ *Greek cargo ships carried oil, wheat and wine for trading. The sailors painted eyes on either side of the prow in the hope they would scare away evil spirits.*

► *A Greek house may have looked like this 2600 years ago, with first-floor bedrooms overlooking a central courtyard.*

- **The early** Greeks loved athletics and held four major events. They were called the Panhellenic Games and drew competitors from all over the Greek world.

- **The four** Panhellenic Games were the Olympic, Pythian, Isthmian and Nemean Games.

- **The Olympic** Games started in 776BC and were the most important. They were held every four years, at Olympia.

- **The Greek** poet Homer wrote his famous poems about the Trojan Wars around 700BC

The Mayans

- **The Mayans** were a people who dominated Central America for 2500 years, until AD1441.

- **The Mayans** began building large pyramids with small temples on top between 600BC and AD250.

- **Mayan** civilization peaked between AD250 and 900. This is known as the Classic Period.

> **⋯ FASCINATING FACT ⋯**
> The Mayans were brilliant astronomers and believed that the stars linked them to their gods.

- **During** the Classic Period, Mayan civilization centred on great cities such as Tikal in the Guatemalan lowlands. They traded far and wide – on foot and also in dug-out canoes.

▲ *The Mayan pyramid at Chichén Itzá, in the Yucatán.*

- **Mayans** in the Classic Period developed a clever form of writing in symbols representing sounds or ideas. They recorded their history on stone monuments called *stelae.*

- **Mysteriously**, around AD800, the Mayans stopped making stelae and the Guatemalan cities were abandoned.

- **From AD800** to 1200, the most powerful Mayan city was Chichén Itzá, in the Yucatán region of modern-day Mexico. From AD1200 to 1440 another city, Mayapan, came to the fore. After 1440, Mayan civilization rapidly broke up, though no one knows why.

- **Mayans** were very religious. Deer, dogs, turkeys and even humans were often sacrificed to the gods in the temples on top of the pyramids.

- **Mayan farmers** grew mainly corn, beans and squash. From the corn, women made flat pancakes now called tortillas, and an alcoholic drink called *balche.*

▶ *The Mayans created complex calendars based on their detailed observation of the stars.*

Confucius

- **Confucius** (said 'con-few-shuss') is the most famous thinker and teacher in Chinese history.

- **Confucius** is the name used by Europeans. Chinese people called him Kongzi or K'ung-Fu-Tzu.

- **Confucius** was born in Lu, now Shantung Province, in 551BC, traditionally on September 28th, and died in 479BC.

- **Confucius** mastered the six Chinese arts – ritual, music, archery, charioteering, calligraphy (writing) and arithmetic – and went on to become a brilliant teacher.

- **Confucius** was the first person in China to argue that all men should be educated in order to make the world a better place, and that teaching could be a way of life.

- **In middle age,** Confucius served as a minister for the King of Lu. He had a highly moral approach to public service. He told statesmen this golden rule: 'Do not do to others what you would not have them do to you.'

- **The King** of Lu was not interested in Confucius' ideas, so Confucius went into exile, followed by his students.

- **After his death,** Confucius' ideas were developed by teachers like Mencius (390-305BC) and Xunzi (c.250BC) into a way of life called Confucianism. Until recently, this dominated Chinese life.

- **Living** at the same time as Confucius may have been a man called Lao-Tse. Lao-Tse wrote the *Tao Te Ching*, the basis of Taoist religion.

- **The *Tao Te Ching*** tells of the Tao (Way) – the underlying unity of nature that makes everything what it is.

78

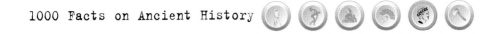

◀ *Little is known about Lao-Tse, the founder of Taoism. Legend has it that while travelling on an ox one day, he was stopped at a border post. There he wrote down his teachings. He then vanished and was never seen again.*

▶ *Confucius' belief was that court officials should not plot for power but study music, poetry and the history of their ancestors.*

79

Chinese technology

- **Western** experts have only recently realized that ancient Chinese technology was very advanced, and many of their early inventions only reached Europe thousands of years later.

- **In the early** AD1600s, the great English thinker Francis Bacon said that three quite recent inventions had changed the world – printing, gunpowder and the ship's magnetic compass. In fact, all of these had been invented in China at a thousand years earlier.

- **One of the** oldest surviving printed books is the *Diamond Sutra*, printed in China about AD868. However, printing in China goes back to at least the 7th century AD.

- **The world's** first robot was an amazing ancient Chinese cart. Gears from the wheels turned a statue on top so that its finger always pointed south.

▲ *Mechanical clocks were invented by the Chinese in AD723 – 600 years earlier than Europe. This is Su Sung's 'Cosmic Engine', an amazing 10-m-high clock built at Khaifeng in AD1090.*

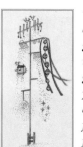

◀ *The Chinese discovered gunpowder and made the first guns about 1100 years ago. They also became famous for their fireworks.*

◀ *In AD132, Chang Heng made the world's first earthquake detector with a special jar. When even a faint, distant quake occurred, a metal ball would fall with a clang from the dragon's mouth at the top of the jar into the toad's mouth.*

◀ *A magnetic compass called a sinan was made by the Chinese over 2000 years ago. A ladle made of a magnetic stone called lodestone spins round on a shiny bronze plate to point south.*

- **The Chinese** had alcoholic spirits 2000 years ago, over a thousand years before they came to Europe.

- **The horse stirrup** was probably invented in China in the 3rd century BC. This gave horse-soldiers a platform to fight from and allowed them to wear armour.

- **The wheelbarrow** was invented by the Chinese c.100BC.

- **Cast-iron** ploughs were made in China c.200BC.

- **Football was** invented in China. About 200BC, they were playing a game called *t'su chu*. It involved kicking an inflated leather ball through a hole in a silk net.

▲ *One particularly nasty Chinese invention was the 'Heaven-Rumbling Thunderclap Fierce Fire Erupter'. This was a gunpowder-fired device that shot out shells of poisonous gas.*

▲ *Water-powered machines for spinning cloth are often thought of as inventions of the English Industrial Revolution in the AD1700s. In fact, the Chinese were building them at least 500 years earlier, to spin a cloth called ramie.*

▶ *Acupuncture involves sticking pins in certain points on the body to treat illness. The Chinese used it 1,800 years ago – but it may have been used earlier in Europe .*

The search for Troy

- **Troy is** the city in the ancient Greek poet Homer's famous epic, the *Iliad*. It was once thought to be entirely mythical.

- **In 1822,** British scholar Charles McClaren suggested that Homer's Troy might be in Turkey. He pinpointed a mound called Hisarlik near the Dardanelles – a narrow sea linking the Black Sea and the Aegean.

- **German** archaeologist Heinrich Schliemann began digging at Hisarlik mound in 1871.

- **In 1873,** Schliemann uncovered fortifications and remains of a very ancient city, which he believed to be Troy.

- **Schliemann** also found a treasure of gold and silver, which he called Priam's treasure after the Trojan king Priam, mentioned in the *Iliad*. He smuggled this out of Turkey to take to Europe.

- **In 1876,** Schliemann was digging at Mycenae in Greece. He came across what he thought was the tomb of Agamemnon – king of the Trojans' enemies in Homer's *Iliad*.

- **In the 1890s,** Wilhelm Dorpfield showed that Hisarlik mound is made of nine layers of city remains. This is because the city was destroyed by fire or earthquake nine times. Each time the survivors built on the rubble.

- **Schliemann** thought Homer's Troy was Troy II (2), second layer from the bottom. Dorpfield thought it was Troy VI.

- **Troy I to V** (1 to 5) are now thought to date from the early Bronze Age (*c.*3000 to 1900BC).

- **Experts** now think Homer's Troy may be Troy VIIa, a layer of the seventh city, dating from about 1250BC.

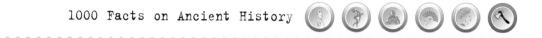

▲ When Schliemann found this gold mask at Mycenae, in 1876, he thought it must be Agamemnon's. In fact, it dates from 300 years earlier.

Greek city-states

- **Ancient** Greece was not a single country in its early days, but a collection of independent cities or city-states.
- **A Greek** city-state was called a *polis* (plural *poleis*).
- *Polis* gives us the words politics and police – and polite.
- **There** were several hundred poleis in ancient Greece. The largest were Athens and Sparta.
- **Each city** typically had a mound called an *acropolis* with a temple on top, and a market place called an *agora*.
- **To start** with (from about 800 to 600BC), city-states were governed by oligarchs (a few powerful men) or a tyrant, but other people gradually got more say in how things were run.
- **People** in Greek city-states were either free or slaves. Free men (not women) were split into citizens (born in the city itself) and *metics* (immigrants).

- **In 508BC,** a man called Cleisthenes gave Athens a new system of government called democracy.

- **Democracy** comes from the Greek word *demos* ('people') and *kratos* ('rule'). The idea was that every citizen (except metics and slaves) had the right to speak and vote in the Assembly, held every ten days on a hill called the Pnyx.

▼ *The most famous acropolis is the Acropolis in Athens with the Parthenon temple on top, but nearly every polis (city-state) had one.*

...FASCINATING FACT...
The laws of the Athenian oligarch Draco were so harsh that severe laws are still called 'draconian'.

The Zhou and Qin

- **c.1100BC,** the Shang in China were conquered by a people called the Zhou.

- **The Zhou** extended the Shang's territory far across China, but the kingdom was divided into large estates, each with its own ruler.

▲ Although today's brick and stone wall dates from the AD1400s, the Great Wall of China was first built of earth bricks in 214BC, under Shi Huangdi.

- **At this** time, the Chinese began using iron for ploughs and weapons, and made advances in technology.

- **Great thinkers** such as Laozi and Confucius came to the fore.

- **Confucius** believed morals were vital in government, but a minister called Shang Yang thought that the law must be strengthened by any means. This is called Legalism.

- **Shang** Yang's family – the Qin – overthrew the Zhou in 312BC.

- **In 246BC,** Qin emperor Zheng expanded the empire and called himself Shi Huangdi, First Emperor. He had the 4000-km-long Great Wall built to protect his empire from nomads from the north.

- **Shi Huangdi** banned books and buried 460 Confucian scholars alive. When His eldest son Fu Su was objected, he was banished.

- **When** Shi Huangdi died, in 210BC, his body was taken secretly to the capital by minister Li Si with a fish cart to hide the smell of rotting flesh. Li Si sent a letter to Fu Su, pretending it was from his father, telling him to commit suicide. Fu Su did and so Li Si came to power.

- **Shi Huangdi** was buried with an army of 6000 life-size clay soldiers, called the Terracotta Army when found in 1974. Certain parts of the tomb are said to be booby-trapped.

▼ *The great tomb of the Terracotta Army (or Warriors) is located near Xi'an, central China. In their underground chambers, the life-size figures are arranged in precise military formation.*

Famous generals

- **In 2300BC**, King Sargon of Akkadia led his soldiers to victory over much larger armies by using especially far-shooting bows.

- **Thutmose III** (1479-1425BC) was perhaps the greatest warrior-pharaoh, fighting 17 campaigns and taking Egypt's empire to its greatest extent.

- **Assurbanipal** (669-627BC) was the great Assyrian leader whose chariots gave him a powerful empire from the Nile to the Caucasus Mountains.

- **Sun-Tzu was** the Chinese military genius who, in 500BC, wrote the first manual on the art of war.

- **Alexander** the Great (356-323BC) was the Macedonian whose army of 35,000 was the most efficient yet seen. He perfected the phalanx (soldiers arranged in very close formation), which proved highly effective in battle.

- **Hannibal** (247-182BC) was the greatest general of the powerful city of Carthage (now near Tunis in Africa).

- **Scipio** (237-183BC) was the Roman general who conquered Spain and broke Carthaginian power in Africa.

- **Julius Caesar** (ca100-44BC) was the greatest Roman general.

- **Belisarius** (AD505-565) and Narses (AD478-573) were generals for Byzantine Emperor Justinian. Their mounted archers defeated the Vandals and Goths.

- **Charles Martel** (AD688-741), 'the Hammer', was the Frankish king who defeated the Moors at Tours in France in AD732 and turned back the Arab conquest of Europe.

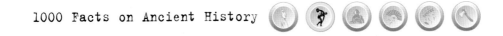

▲ *Hannibal's greatest feat was leading an army – with elephants – through Spain and then the Alps, in winter, to attack Rome from the north.*

89

Buddha

- **Buddha** was the founder of the Buddhist religion, who was living in India c.563-483BC.

- **Buddha's** real name was Siddhartha Gautama.

- **Buddha** is not a name but a title (like 'the messiah') meaning 'enlightened one', so you should really say 'the Buddha'.

- **Archaeological** excavations finished in 1995 suggest that a man who may have been Siddhartha lived in the palace of his father Suddodhana on what is now the border of Nepal and India.

- **As a young** prince, Siddhartha lived a life of luxury. When he was 16 years old, he married his cousin the Princess Yasodhara, who was also 16 years old.

▼ *Young Buddhist monks in traditional orange robes. They are taught to follow eight steps towards truth and wisdom.*

- **The turning** point was when Siddhartha was 29 and he saw four visions: an old man, a sick man, a corpse and a wandering holy man.

- **The first** three visions told Siddhartha that life involved ageing, sickness and death. The fourth told him he must leave his wife and become a holy man.

- **After six years** of self-denial, Siddhartha sat down under a shady 'bo' tree to think – and after several hours great wisdom came to him.

- **The Buddha** spent the rest of his life preaching his message around India.

- **The Buddha** died at the age of 80. His bones became sacred relics.

▶ *Most statues of the Buddha show him sitting cross-legged, in deep meditation (thought).*

Greek thinkers

▲ *Euclid, great Greek mathematician and author of the 13-volume work,* Elements, *was teaching in Alexandria around 300BC.*

● **The great** thinkers of ancient Greece were called philosophers. *Philosophy* is Greek for 'love of wisdom'.

● **The key** philosophers were Socrates, Plato and Aristotle.

● **Socrates** (466-399BC) believed people would behave well if they knew what good behaviour was and challenged people to think about truth, good and evil.

● **Plato** (427-348BC) argued that, behind the messy chaos of everyday experience, there is a perfect and beautiful Idea or Form. He also tried to find the ideal way of governing a state.

● **Aristotle** (384-322BC) argued that, for true knowledge, you must find the 'final cause' – why something happens.

● **Aristotle** was the first great scientist, stressing the need to collect data, sort the results and interpret them.

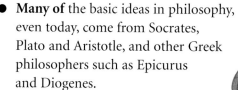

- **Many of** the basic ideas in philosophy, even today, come from Socrates, Plato and Aristotle, and other Greek philosophers such as Epicurus and Diogenes.

- **Greek** mathematicians such as Euclid, Appolonius, Pythagoras and Archimedes worked out many of our basic rules of maths. Most school geometry still depends on the system devised by Euclid.

- **Greek** astronomers like Aristarchus and Anaxagoras made many brilliant deductions – but many of these were forgotten. Aristarchus realized that the Earth turned on its axis and circled the Sun. Yet it was almost 2000 years before this idea was generally accepted.

▲ *Aristotle, the brilliant tutor to Alexander the Great, was thought of as the ultimate authority on every subject for over 2000 years.*

> ...**FASCINATING FACT**...
> Archimedes showed how the effect of a lever could be worked out by maths.

Homer

- **Homer** is the ancient Greek poet said to have written the ancient world's two greatest poems: the *Iliad* and the *Odyssey*.

- **Homer** probably lived in the 9th century BC in Ionia, on what is now the Aegean coast of Turkey, or on the island of Chios.

- **No one** knows for certain if Homer actually existed, or if he composed all of both poems. Most current experts think that he did.

- **In Homer's** time there was a great tradition of bards. These were poets who recited aloud great tales of heroic deeds. They knew the poems by heart and so never wrote them down.

- **The *Iliad*** and the *Odyssey* are the only poems from the times of the bards that were written down and so survive. They may have been written down at the time, or later.

- **After Homer's** time, the two great poems were used in religious festivals in Greece.

- **For centuries** after Homer's time, Greek children learned to read, and learned about the legends of the past, by studying Homer's two great poems.

- **In the 2nd** century BC, scholars at the Alexandrian Library in Egypt studied the poems. A few scholars came to the conclusion that they were so different in style they must have been written by two different poets.

▲ *Nothing is known for certain about Homer, but legend says that he was blind.*

- **The *Iliad*** is a long poem in lofty language about the Trojan Wars, in which the Greeks besiege the city of Troy to take back the kidnapped Helen.

- **The *Odyssey*** tells of a great journey made by hero Odysseus, and his adventures along the way.

▶ The Odyssey *recounts the adventures of Odysseus on his 10-year journey home after the war against Troy. In one tragic scene, Odysseus's faithful old dog Argus dies as his master reaches his home town.*

Early Americans

- **The Americas** were the last continents that humans occupied.

- **The first** Americans may have been Australian aboriginals who arrived by boat 50,000 years ago.

- **Ancestors** of today's Native Americans probably came to the Americas 20-35,000 years ago, from Asia. They are thought to have walked across the strip of land that once joined Asia and North America across the Bering Strait.

- **By 6000BC,** the first Native Americans had spread south from Alaska and far down into South America.

- **There is** evidence that humans were living in Mexico over 20,000 years ago. At El Jobo in Colombia, South America, pendants dating back to 14,920BC have been found.

- **10,000 years** ago, groups of 'Paleo-Indians' on North America's Great Plains hunted now-extinct animals such as camels and mammoths. In the dry western mountains, desert peoples planted wild grass-seed.

▲ *Large woolly mammoths originated in Africa and were related to elephants. Native Americans hunted them for their hide and flesh.*

- **In Mexico,** people began to grow squash, peppers and beans at least 8500 years ago.

- **Corn** (maize) was probably first grown in Mexico, about 7000 years ago.

- **Corn,** beans and squash provided food for early American civilizations such as the Olmecs and Mayans.

> **...FASCINATING FACT...**
> A 50,000-year-old skull found in Colombia resembles the skulls of Australian aboriginals.

▼ *Carving wooden duck decoys for hunting is a North American tradition dating back thousands of years.*

▲ *The name 'squash' comes from the Indian word 'kutasquash', which means raw or uncooked. Squash is still a widely grown vegetable today.*

Greek art

- **In the heyday** of ancient Greece, thousands of sculptors, architects, painters, dramatists and poets were creating a fantastic wealth of beautiful works of art.

- **The Greeks** made graceful statues and friezes to decorate temples and homes. They were carved mostly from marble and limestone and then painted, though in surviving statues the paint has worn away.

- **The most** famous sculptors were Phidias (*c.*490-420BC), Praxiteles (*c.*330BC), Lysippus (*c.*380-306BC) and Myron (*c.*500-440BC). Phidias's huge gold and ivory statue of the god Zeus was famed throughout the ancient world.

- **Greek** architects such as Ictinus and Callicrates created beautiful marble and limestone temples fronted by graceful columns and elegant triangular friezes. The most famous is the Parthenon in Athens.

- **The Greeks** had three styles for columns: the simple Doric, the slender Ionic, topped by scrolls, and the ornate Corinthian, topped by sculpted acanthus leaves.

- **The style** created by the Greek temples is now called Classical and has influenced architects ever since.

- **The Greeks** believed that different arts (such as dance or poetry) were inspired by one of nine goddesses, who were known as the Muses.

- **Ancient Greek** writers include the poets Homer, Sappho and Pindar. They created styles of writing that included epic poetry – long, dramatic tales of heroic deeds.

▲ *The famous Venus de Milo was found on the Aegean island of Milos in AD1820. It was carved in Greek Antioch (now in Turkey) around 150BC and shows the goddess of love, Aphrodite (Roman goddess Venus). The statue originally had arms.*

- **The tragedy** is a grand drama doomed to end unhappily for the hero. Tragedy was created by Greek dramatists such as Aeschylus, Euripides and Sophocles, who wrote the tragedy *King Oedipus*.

> ....**FASCINATING FACT**....
> The Colossus of Rhodes was a huge 37-m-high statue cast in bronze by Greek sculptor Chares. It stood near to the harbour of Rhodes, an island in the Aegean Sea.

A typical theatre, like the Theatre of Dionysus in Athens, seated 14,000 in stadium-like rows

A 'chorus' of actors linked the scenes with verse and songs

The circular acting area was called the *orchestra*

Scenes were played by just two or three actors, each wearing a mask

Behind the *orchestra* was a house or *skene*, where the actors changed. Later, this became a backdrop

Audiences took cushions to sit on and picnics to sustain them through very long plays

▶ *Formal drama was developed in ancient Greece in the 5th and 6th centuries BC. Huge audiences watched plays in open-air arenas.*

In later Greek theatres, the *skene* developed side wings here called *paraskinia*

What people ate

- **1.5 million years** ago, people learned how to use fire to cook food. The oldest known cooking fire is at Swartkrans, South Africa.

- **The first** ovens were pits for hot coals, first used in the Ukraine about 20,000 years ago. The first real ovens were from Sumer and Egypt, *c.*2600BC.

- **Grain seeds** were cooked and mixed with water to make gruel (porridge). Around 20,000 years ago, people learned to bake gruel on a hot stone to make flat bread, like pitta.

- **The development** of pottery meant that liquids could be heated to make stews. The oldest pottery is 13,000-year-old pots from Odai-Yamomoto in Japan. The first pots from the Near East, from Iran, date back 11,000 years.

◀ *Romans used to go to cheap eating houses called 'popinae' for their main meals. Here they could buy bread, cheese, fruit and cheap cuts of meat. Only the rich could afford to employ a chef to prepare meals.*

- *c.*12,000 years ago, people found how to make food last by letting it ferment, making cheese from milk and wine from grapes.

- *c.*8000BC, people began to farm animals such as sheep and grow plants such as cereals for food. Diets became less varied than when people gathered wild food, but much more reliable.

- *c.*4000BC, special farmers in Palestine were growing oil-rich olives to squeeze and make olive oil in huge amounts. Romans consumed vast quantities.

- *c.*2600BC, the Egyptians found that, by leaving gruel to ferment, they could make a dough. They baked this in ovens to make the first raised bread.

- **Honey** was the main sweetener. Egyptians kept bees for honey and also made sweet syrups from fruits.

- **The oldest** recipe book is an Assyrian stone tablet dating from 1700BC that features 25 recipes, including a bird called a tarru cooked in onion, garlic, milk and spices.

▶ *Bread was the first processed food, made by baking ground-up grass seeds mixed with water.*

▶ *The earliest people simply ate what food they could find – either by hunting (like fish) or gathering (like berries).*

101

The Phoenicians

- **From about** 3000BC, Semitic peoples such as Canaanites lived on the eastern Mediterranean coast and built the great city of Byblos.

- **From about** 1100BC, the people living here became known as Phoenicians.

- **The word** 'phoenicians' comes from *phoinix*, the Greek word for a purple dye made famous by these people.

- **The Phoenicians** were great sea traders. Their ports, of Tyre and Sidon, bustled with ships carrying goods from all over the known world.

- **The Phoenicians** used wool from Mesopotamia and flax and linen from Egypt to make cloth. They also made jewellery from imported gems, metals and ivory.

- **Phoenicians** invented the alphabet and gave us the word 'too'. The Phoenician words *aleph* ('ox') and *beth* ('house') became the Greek letters alpha and beta. The word 'bible' and the prefix 'bibli-' (meaning 'books') come from the city of Byblos.

- **The dye** for which the Phoenicians were famous was made from the shells of Murex snails.

- *c.*600BC, Phoenician sailors sailed from the Red Sea right round Africa and back into the Mediterranean.

- **Phoenicians** set up colonies across the Mediterranean as far west as Gades (now Cadiz, in Spain).

  - **The greatest** Phoenician colony was the city of Carthage in what is now Tunisia.

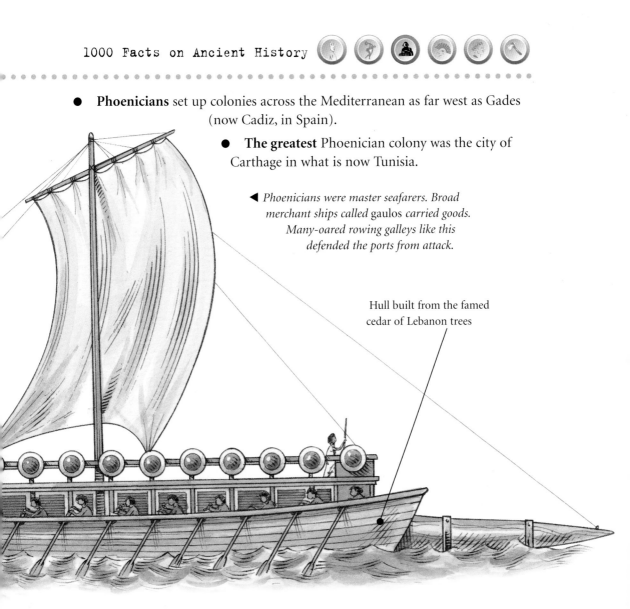

◀ *Phoenicians were master seafarers. Broad merchant ships called* gaulos *carried goods. Many-oared rowing galleys like this defended the ports from attack.*

Hull built from the famed cedar of Lebanon trees

Polynesians

- **Polynesians** are the peoples who live on the many islands in the middle of the Pacific Ocean, from Hawaii to Easter Island and New Zealand.

- **There are** 10,000 islands in Polynesia and the rest of the eastern Pacific, with hundreds of different cultures and languages, each with its own history.

- **Many Polynesian** islands may well have been first settled 40,000 years ago by people from Southeast Asia.

- **2000 years ago,** a second wave of migrants moved east from Fiji, Samoa and Tonga to the Marquesas Islands.

◀ Outriggers are a traditional boat of Polynesia, and are named after rigging that sticks out to the sides to aid stability. Easy to pull ashore, and perfect for shallow waters, these were ideal boats for island life.

- **The settlers** crossed the ocean in small double canoes and boats called outriggers.

- **In their** canoes the settlers took crops (coconuts, yams, taros and breadfruit) and livestock (pigs and chickens).

- **Every island** developed its own style of woodcarving.

- **About AD400,** the new Polynesians moved on to Hawaii and Easter Island.

- **Easter Islanders** created strange stone statues called *moais*, carved with stone tools since they had no metal.

▼ *There are about 600 huge stone moai statues on Easter Island, on platforms called ahus. No one knows what they were for.*

Greek mythology

- **The Greeks** had a wealth of myths – stories about their gods, goddesses, heroes and villains.

- **We know** about the myths mainly from Homer's poems and Hesiod's book *Theogeny*, both from about 700BC.

- *Theogeny* tells how the Earth began, with the earth goddess Gaia emerging from chaos and giving birth to Uranus, the king of the sky.

- **The many** children of Gaia and Uranus were called the Titans, led by Cronos.

- **Cronos** married his sister Rhea. Their children, led by Zeus, rebelled against the Titans to become the new top gods, called the Olympians.

- **The Olympians** were said to live on Mount Olympus, and include the most famous Greek gods, such as Apollo the god of light, Demeter the goddess of crops, Artemis the goddess of the Moon and Dionysius the wine god.

◀ ▲ *Many Greek gods were adopted by the Romans. The winged messenger Hermes (above) became Mercury in ancient Rome, while Aphrodite, the goddess of love (left), became Venus.*

- **Greek heroes** were mostly those who had performed great deeds during the times of the Trojan Wars or earlier.

- **Early** heroes include Jason, who led his Argonauts (his crew) in search of the fabulous Golden Fleece, and Theseus, who killed the Minotaur.

- **Trojan** war heroes included Achilles and Odysseus.

- **The greatest** hero was super-strong Heracles, whom the Romans would later call Hercules.

▶ *King of the Greek gods was Zeus. He ruled from his home on Mount Olympus and headed a group of Greek gods called the Olympians. Zeus is a weather and sky god and is especially associated with thunder and lightning. The Roman god Jupiter is the equivalent to Zeus.*

Alexander the Great

- **Alexander** the Great was a young Macedonian king who was one of the greatest generals in history. He built an empire stretching from Greece to India.

- **Alexander** was born in 356BC in Pella, capital of Macedonia. His father, King Phillip II, was a tough fighter who conquered neighbouring Greece. His mother was the fiery Olympias, who told him that he was descended from Achilles, the hero of the *Iliad*.

Alexander the Great

- **As a boy,** he was tutored by the famous philosopher Aristotle. A story tells how he tamed the unridable ho Bucephalus, which afterwards carried him as far as India.

- **When** Alexander was 20, his father was murdered by a bodyguard and he became king. Alexander quickly stamped out rebellion.

- **In 334BC,** Alexander crossed the narrow neck of sea separating Europe from Asia with his army. Within a year, he had conquered the mighty Persian Empire.

- **In 331BC,** Alexander led his army into Egypt, where he was made pharaoh and founded the city of Alexandria. He trekked to the desert oasis of Siwah, where legend says an oracle proclaimed him son of the Greek god Zeus.

◀ *The key to Macedonian success was the phalanx – armoured soldiers standing in tightly packed rows bristling with long spears. Such a formation could withstand a cavalry attack, yet still move swiftly.*

108

- **In 327BC,** he married the lovely Bactrian princess, Roxane.

- **After capturing** the city of
Babylon and finishing off
the Persian king, Darius,
Alexander led his conquering
army into India. Here his
homesick troops finally asked
to go home.

> ...FASCINATING FACT...
> An old legend said that anyone who
> untied a tricky knot in a town called
> Gordium would conquer Asia.
> Alexander instantly sliced through this
> Gordian knot with his sword.

- **In 325BC,** Alexander had ships
built and carried his army down the Indus River and
returned to Babylon. Within a year, he fell ill and died.

▶ *In just nine years
and a series of
brilliant campaigns,
Alexander created a
vast empire. No one
knows exactly what
his plans were.
However, the
teachings of his
tutor Aristotle were
important to him,
and he had his own
vision of different
peoples living
together in
friendship.*

Macedonia
Gordium
Samarkand
Mediterranean
Alexandria
Syria
Egypt
Babylon
Persia
Hindu Kush
Persepolis
Indus River
India
Indian Ocean
Alexander's route

The birth of Rome

- **People were living** in Italy long before Rome was founded and a people called the Etruscans created an advanced civilization in the northwest between 800 and 400BC.

- **According** to legend, Rome was founded in 753BC by the twins Romulus and Remus, who were said to have been brought up by a she-wolf.

- **By 550BC,** Rome was a big city ruled by Etruscan kings.

- **In 509BC,** the Roman people drove out the kings and formed themselves into an independent republic.

▲ Senators were men from leading citizen families who had served the Roman republic as judges or state officials. They made new laws and discussed government plans.

▲ The first rules of the Roman legal system were recorded in 450BC in a document called the Twelve Tables. The Roman system forms the basis of many legal systems today.

▶ *Legend has it that after founding the city of Rome, Romulus and Remus quarrelled and Romulus killed his brother.*

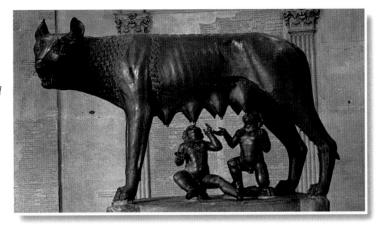

- **Republican** Rome was ruled by the Senate, an assembly made up of 100 patricians (men from leading families).

- **In theory,** Rome was governed by the people. However, real power was in the hands of patricians; plebeians (ordinary citizens) had little. Slaves had no power or rights at all.

- **Plebeians** fought for power and, by 287BC, gained the right to stand as consuls, the highest official posts.

- **In the 400s** and 300s BC, Rome extended its power all over Italy, by both brute force and alliances.

- **By 264BC,** Rome rivalled Carthage, the North African city that dominated the western Mediterranean. In 164BC, Rome destroyed Carthage totally after the Punic Wars.

- **By 130BC,** Rome had built a mighty empire stretching from Spain to Turkey and along the North African coast.

Cleopatra

- **Cleopatra** (69-30BC) was the last Macedonian queen of Egypt. She was descended from Ptolemy, a general of Alexander the Great who made himself king after Alexander died.

- **Cleopatra** may have been beautiful. She was certainly intelligent, charming and highly determined.

- **Cleopatra** became queen in 51BC, when her father died. Her ten-year-old brother Ptolemy became king.

- **Ptolemy's** guardians seized power and drove Cleopatra out. She was restored to the throne by the Roman armies of Julius Caesar.

- **Legend** has it that Cleopatra had herself delivered to Caesar rolled up in a carpet. Whatever the truth, Caesar fell in love with her, and she had a son, Caesarion, by him.

▲ *Octavian described Cleopatra as a wicked temptress – and the idea has stuck. Her people in Egypt, however, thought of her as a great, just and much-loved queen.*

- **Caesar** invited Cleopatra and Caesarion to Rome, where she stayed until 44BC, when Caesar was brutally assassinated.

- **The Roman** general Mark Antony went to Cleopatra for her support in his bid for power in Rome. He too fell in love with her. They later married and had three children.

- **Mark Antony** returned to Rome to make a political marriage to Octavia, sister of Octavian. However, he soon returned to Cleopatra.

- **Mark Antony** and Cleopatra were ambitious and strove to take over the eastern Roman Empire. Their armies, however, were defeated at the Battle of Actium, off Greece, in 31BC by the forces of Octavian (later known as Augustus Caesar).

- **As Octavian** chased them to Alexandria, Cleopatra spread rumours that she was dead. In despair, Mark Antony stabbed himself. He died in her arms. Cleopatra tried to make peace with Octavian but failed. She took her life by placing an asp, a poisonous snake, on her breast.

▶ *Much is made of Mark Antony and Cleopatra's romantic relationship, but theirs was also a strong political alliance.*

113

Rome on the rise

- **As Rome's** empire spread, the creation of plantations worked by slaves put small farmers out of work. The gap between rich and poor widened.

- **Many joined** the army to escape poverty and became more loyal to their generals than to the Senate (the government's ruling body).

- **Two popular** generals, Pompey and Julius Caesar, used their armies to take over Rome and suspend the Republic.

- **Caesar** and Pompey argued, and after battles right across the empire, Caesar gained the upper hand.

- **Once in** power, Caesar restored order and passed laws to reduce people's debts.

- **Caesar** was made dictator and ruled Rome without the Senate.

▼ *Wealthy Romans owned slaves to cater to every whim. Slaves that did very well, however, could win their freedom.*

- **In 44BC,** a man called Brutus killed Caesar to restore the Republic – but Caesar's place was taken by another general, Octavian, Caesar's adopted son.

- **By 27BC,** Octavian was so powerful he declared himself the first Roman emperor and took the name Augustus.

- **Under** Augustus, rebellious parts of Spain and the Alps were brought under control and the empire was expanded along the Rhine and Danube Rivers.

- **By 1BC,** the days of strife were over and Rome presided over a vast, stable, prosperous empire.

▲ *Many Romans lived in comfortable two-storey townhouses (*domi*), with heated pools and underfloor heating.*

Jesus Christ

- **Jesus Christ** was one of the world's great religious leaders. The religion of Christianity is based on his teachings.

- **Our knowledge** of Jesus's life comes almost entirely from four short books in the Bible's New Testament: the gospels of Matthew, Mark, Luke and John.

- **Roman** writers such as Pliny mention Jesus briefly.

- **Jesus** was born in Bethlehem, Palestine, between 4 and 1BC.

▼ *The site of Jesus's birth, now called the Church of the Nativity, can be found in the heart of Bethlehem. A silver star marks the exact place where Jesus was born.*

- **The Bible** tells how his poor young virgin mother, Mary, became miraculously pregnant after a visit by the archangel Gabriel, and that Jesus is the only Son of God.

- **Little is** known of Jesus's childhood. His teaching began after he was baptized by John the Baptist at the age of 30.

- **Jesus's mission** was to announce that the Kingdom of God was coming. From his many followers, he chose 12 'apostles' to help him spread the word.

- **Jesus** is said to have performed all kinds of miracles to convince people of the truth of his teachings.

- **Many Jews** felt Jesus was a troublemaker, especially after a triumphal entry into Jerusalem. They had the Roman governor, Pontius Pilate, put him to death by crucifixion (nailing to a cross).

.....FASCINATING FACT...
After his death, Jesus was said to have been resurrected – brought to life again.

▶ *The word 'Christ' is actually a title. It comes from the Greek word* christos, *which means 'anointed one'.*

The Han dynasty

- **In 210BC,** the small Han kingdom was ruled over by Liu Bang. Liu Bang was a poor villager who had come to power as the Qin Empire broke down.

- **In 206BC,** Liu Bang led an army on the Qin capital, Xiangyang. He looted Shi Huangdi's tomb, and burned the city and the library containing the books Shi Huangdi had banned – the only existing copies.

- **In 202BC,** Liu Bang proclaimed himself to be the first Han emperor and took the name Gaozu.

- **Under** the Han, China became as large and powerful as the Roman Empire; art and science thrived. Chinese people still sometimes call themselves Han.

- **Under** Wudi (141-87BC), Han China reached its peak.

- **Han cities** were huge, crowded and beautiful, and craftsmen made many exquisite things from wood, paint and silk. Sadly, many of these lovely objects were destroyed when Han rule ended.

- **Silk, jade** and horses were traded along the Silk Route, which wound through Asia as far as the Roman Empire.

- **Han emperors** tried to recover the lost writings and revived the teachings of Confucius. Public officials became scholars and in 165BC the first exams for entry into public service were held.

- **About AD50,** Buddhist missionaries reached China.

- **By AD200,** the Han emperors were weakened by their ambitious wives and eunuchs (guardians). Rebellions by a group called the Yellow Turbans, combined with attacks by warriors from the north, brought the empire down.

▶ *Beautiful objects like this bronze urn were traded between China and Europe along the famous Silk Route for thousands of years.*

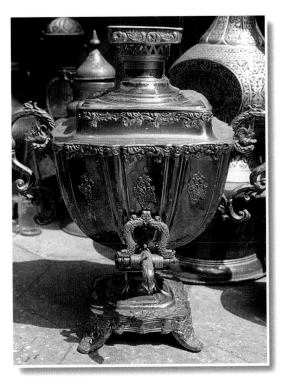

▼ *Richly coloured silks were bought from Chinese merchants by traders from ancient Persia (modern day Iran). Silk was also transported from China by camel trains to Damascus, gateway between the East and West.*

Roman towns

- **Roman** towns were the biggest and most sophisticated the world had seen. They were not built on rigid grids like Greek cities, but they all had common features.

- **Roman** towns had two main streets and many side streets with spaces in between called *insulae* (islands).

▲ *The remains of the forum in Rome give a glimpse of just how magnificent Roman cities must have been.*

- **The insulae** were tightly packed with private houses – houses of the rich, called *domi*, and apartment blocks (also called *insulae*). The bigger Roman houses had courtyards.

- **Traffic** jams were so common that many towns banned wheeled traffic from the streets during daylight.

- **Most towns** had numerous shops, inns (*tabernae*), cafés (*thermopilia*) and bakeries (*pistrina*).

- **The forum** was a large open market and meeting place surrounded on three sides by a covered walkway. On the fourth side was the law courts and the town hall (*basilica*).

120

- **Most towns** had many grand temples to Roman gods.

- **Most towns** had a large open-air theatre. There was also a games arena, or stadium, where warriors called gladiators fought and chariot races were held.

- **The bath** houses (*thermae*) were places where people came to sit around and dip into hot and cold baths in magnificent surroundings.

- **Towns** had highly sophisticated water supplies and sewage systems.

▼ *The Roman town of Ostia had blocks of flats called 'insulae'. A typical block was three or four storeys high with up to one hundred small, dirty, crowded rooms.*

121

The Roman Empire

- **For 200 years** after Augustus became emperor in 27BC, Roman emperors ruled over an empire so large and secure that citizens could talk of the Pax Romana (Roman Peace).

- **The Romans** built straight roads to move their troops about quickly. On the whole, they governed peacefully and also built hundreds of towns in the Roman manner.

- **After Augustus** died, in AD14, his stepson Tiberius succeeded him. Then came a succession of Augustus's descendants, including Gaius, Claudius and Nero.

> ...**FASCINATING FACT**...
> Roman historian Suetonius claimed that Nero sang and played the lyre during Rome's great fire in AD64.

- **Gaius** (AD37-41) was known as Caligula ('little boots') because of the soldiers' boots he wore as a child.

- **Soon** after Caligula became emperor, an illness left him mad. He spent wildly, had people whipped and killed, married and murdered his sister and elected his horse as a minister. Eventually he was murdered by soldiers.

- **Claudius** (AD41-54) replaced Caligula. People thought he was stupid because he stuttered and was physically disabled. However, he proved the wisest and most humane of all emperors.

◀ *Gladiators were prisoners and criminals who were made to fight in big arenas called amphitheatres to entertain people.*

▶ *The orange area of this map shows the empire at its peak under the Emperor Trajan (AD98-117). It was divided into areas called provinces, such as Britannia (England and Wales) and Gallia (northern France). Each had its own Roman governor, often a retired consul (minister), who used his power to extort taxes.*

▼ *Leading imperial officials wore distinctive flowing robes called togas. Laws were written on papyrus or parchment.*

- **Claudius** was probably poisoned by his fourth wife Agrippina, who wanted power for her son Nero.

- **The power** of Roman emperors reached a peak under the 'Antonines' – Nerva, Trajan, Hadrian, Antoninus and Marcus Aurelius. They ruled AD96-180.

- **The Roman** empire grew only a little after Augustus's death. Britain was conquered in AD43, and Emperor Trajan took Dacia (now Hungary and Romania).

123

The Roman army

- **Rome** owed its power to its highly efficient army.

- **In a crisis,** Rome could raise an army of 800,000 men.

- **The Roman** army fought mainly on foot, advancing in tight squares bristling with spears and protected by large shields called *scutari*. They often put shields over their heads to protect them from arrows. This formation was called a *testudo* – or 'tortoise'.

- **Under** the Republic, the army was divided into legions of 5000 soldiers. Legions were made up of 10 cohorts. Cohorts, in turn, consisted of centuries containing 80-100 soldiers.

- **Each legion** was led by a *legatus*. A cohort was led by a *tribunus militum*. A century was led by a *centurion*.

- **All Roman** soldiers had a short sword (60 cm long) and carried two throwing spears. They also wore armour – first, vests of chain mail and a leather helmet; later, metal strips on a leather tunic and a metal helmet.

- **Roman** armies built huge siege engines and catapults when they had to capture a town.

- **After 100BC,** most Roman soldiers were professionals, who joined the army for life. Food accounted for about a third of their wages.

- **In training,** soldiers went on forced 30-km marches three times a month. They moved at 8 km per hour, carrying very heavy packs.

- **Soldiers** were flogged for misbehaviour. Mutiny was punished by executing one in ten suspects. This was called *decimation.*

◄ *The* testudo *formation proved itself highly effective for Roman foot-soldiers.*

► *Roman soldiers had to be tough – while on the march they carried all their weapons and armour, plus a pack full of clothes, food and tools for digging and building.*

125

How Romans lived

- **In big** cities, rich Romans had a comfortable way of life.

- **For breakfast,** Romans typically ate bread or wheat biscuits with honey, dates or olives, and water or wine.

- **A Roman** lunch (*prandium*) consisted of much the same things as breakfast.

- **Romans** had *cena* (the main meal) in the afternoon, typically after a visit to the baths. This became a very lavish affair with three main courses, and each course had many dishes.

- **Rich Romans** had a lot of free time, since slaves did all the work. Leisure activities included gambling by tossing coins (*capita et navia*) and knucklebones (*tali*).

- **Public** entertainments were called *ludi* (games). They included theatre, chariot races, and fights with gladiators (trained fighters) and animals.

- **The Emperor** Trajan went to a gladiator contest that lasted 117 days and involved 10,000 gladiators.

- **Romans** had more slaves than any empire in history. Many were treated cruelly, but some lived quite well.

- **Between 73-71 BC,** a man called Spartacus led a revolt of slaves that lasted two years, until it was crushed by Roman armies.

▶ *Romans were very clean and spent many hours at public baths or bathing at home. These are the Roman baths at Bath, England.*

126

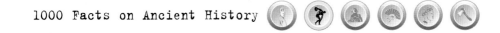

Famous disasters

- **Many ancient** civilizations had legends of great floods.

- **In the Middle** East, a Sumerian named Ziusudra, the Babylonian Gilgamesh and the Jewish Noah all built an ark (boat) to ride out a flood that drowned everyone else.

- **In India,** Manu, the first man and first king, was warned of great flooding by fish and survived by building a boat.

- **In the Americas,** the Aztecs believed four previous worlds had been destroyed by jaguars, hurricanes, thunder and lightning and a huge, 52-year flood.

- **The huge** eruption of the Aegean island volcano of Thera (Santorini), in 1500BC, effectively destroyed Minoan civilization on Crete – and may have started legends of the lost civilization of Atlantis, drowned by a tidal wave.

- **While** the Jews were slaves there, Egypt was ruined by a flood of blood that had been predicted by the Jew Moses – now thought to have been the Nile River in flood, stained by red algae.

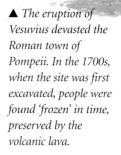

▲ *The eruption of Vesuvius devasted the Roman town of Pompeii. In the 1700s, when the site was first excavated, people were found 'frozen' in time, preserved by the volcanic lava.*

128

- **In 464BC**, 10,000 people were killed by an earthquake that rocked the Greek city of Sparta.

- **In 436BC**, a famine drove thousands of Romans to jump into the Tiber River to escape the pain of starvation.

- **In AD64**, the Rome of Emperor Nero was destroyed by a great fire. Angry people said that Nero had started it.

- **In AD79**, the Roman city of Pompeii was buried under ash from nearby volcano Vesuvius – and preserved to this day.

▼ *The Greek island of Santorini was blown apart in 1500BC by a giant volcanic eruption, so ending the Minoan civilization.*

Yamato

- **The oldest** signs of farming in Japan date back to 300BC, but Japan was inhabited long before that.

- **The first** known inhabitants of Japan were the Ainu or Ezo, who were short, hairy, fair-skinned people. Some Ainu people still survive in northern Japan.

- **About 250BC,** the Yayoi people became dominant in Japan. They used objects made of iron and bronze.

- **Around 660BC,** Jimmu Tenno, the legendary first emperor of Japan, established power in Yamato.

- **Jimmu Tenno** is said to be the descendent of the sun goddess Amaterasu.

- **From AD200-645,** the Yamato dynasty dominated Japan.

- **Right up** to today, Japanese emperors claim to be descended from the Yamato. The Yamato, in turn, claimed to be descended from the Shinto sun-goddess, Amaterasu.

- **Shotoku** Taishi (AD574-622) was a young regent for old Empress Suiko. He gave Japan organized, Chinese-style government and promoted both Buddhism and Confucianism.

- **Shinto** or 'way of the gods' has been Japan's main religion since prehistoric times. It gained its name during the 6th century AD, to distinguish it from Buddhism and Confucianism.

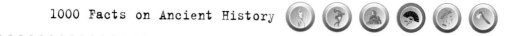

> ...**FASCINATING FACT**...
> In AD2000, the postholes of a round
> hut half a million years old were
> found in Japan.

◄ *Shinto priests*
believe that all
things that inspire
awe – from twisted
trees to dead
warriors – can have
kami *(spirits).*

131

The Mauryan Empire

- **In 321BC,** the first great Indian empire was created by Chandragupta Maurya (*c.*325-297BC). Its capital was Pataliputra on the Ganges.

- **The Mauryan** Empire at its peak included most of modern Pakistan, Bangladesh and India – except for the very southern tip.

- **The most** famous of the Mauryan emperors was Chandragupta's grandson, Asoka (*c.*265-238BC).

- **After witnessing** an horrific battle, Asoka was so appalled by the suffering that he resolved never to go to war. Instead, Asoka devoted himself to improving the lot of his people.

- **Asoka became** a Buddhist and his government promoted the Dharma, or 'Universal Law'.

▲ *Banyan trees have many trunks, each originating from its branches. They were planted to provide shade for travellers along newly built roads.*

- **The Universal Law** preached religious tolerance, non-violence and respect for the dignity of every single person.

- **Asoka's** men dug wells and built reservoirs all over India to help the poor. They also provided comfortable rest-houses and planted shady banyan trees for travellers along the new roads.

- **Asoka** said 'all men are my children', and sent officials out to deal with local problems.

- **A vast secret** police force and an army of 700,000 helped Asoka to run his empire.

- **Asoka's** Sarnath lion insignia is now India's national emblem.

◀ *During Asoka's reign, stupas – domed shrines said to contain relics of the Buddha – were built all over India.*

133

Early North America

- **Maize** (or sweetcorn) was grown in southwestern USA *c.*2000-1000BC.

- **The first** farming villages in the southwest were those of the Anasazi, Mogollon and Hohokam peoples and dated from AD100. They lived either in caves or in underground 'pit houses' carved into the desert rock.

- *Anasazi* is Navajo Indian for 'Ancient Ones'.

- **The first** Anasazi are also known as Basket-Makers because of their skill in weaving baskets.

- **About AD700,** the Anasazi began to build large stone villages called *pueblos,* which is why from this time they are also called Pueblo Indians.

> ...**FASCINATING FACT**...
> Cliff Palace in Mesa Verde (Colorado) had space for 250 people in its 217 rooms.

- **In the 'Classic'** Pueblo period, from AD1050-1300, the Anasazi lived in huge apartments carved out of cliffs, like Pueblo Bonito. Pueblo culture began to fade *c.*AD1300.

- **In the east,** the first farming villages were those of the Hopewell peoples of the Illinois and Ohio valleys, between 100BC and AD200.

- **The Hopewell** people are known for their burial mounds. Things found in these mounds show they traded all over America.

- **About AD700,** farming villages with temple mounds developed near St Louis on the Mississippi River.

▶ *The most famous cliff pueblos are in Mesa Verde, Colorado.*

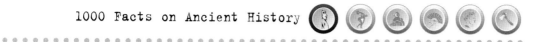

The early Irish

- **Ireland** was settled late. The first proof of settlers are 8000-year-old flints left by hunters and fishermen on beaches in the northeast, near the modern Irish town of Larne.

- **The New** Stone Age (Neolithic) began when the first farms and permanent homes appeared, 5000 years ago.

- **Neolithic** people honoured their dead with long mounds or barrows – called 'court graves' because they have a courtyard at the entrance. They also built barrows called portal graves with three huge stones set like a door.

- **The most** dramatic remains from earliest times are 'passage' graves. Inside an earth mound, a long passage leads to a stone chamber. Of 150 in Ireland, the most famous is Newgrange, in the Boyne valley near Dublin.

- **The Celts** invaded Ireland in the Iron Age, about 400BC, and many of Ireland's rich collection of heroic myths are probably based in this time.

- **Celtic Ireland** was split into 150 kingdoms or clans called *tuatha* and later into five provinces – Ulster, Meath, Leinster, Munster and Connaught. After AD500, there was a high king (*ard-ri*) ruling Ireland from Tara in Leinster.

- **Irish Celts** were both warriors and herdsmen who valued cows highly. They also revered poets (*file*), and their metalwork, revealed in items such as the Tara brooch and the Ardagh chalice, is extraordinarily beautiful.

- **Early Celtic** priests were druids, but legend says that in AD432, St Patrick came to convert Ireland to Christianity.

- **Irish monasteries** became havens of art and learning in the Dark Ages, creating the famous *Book of Kells*.

> **...FASCINATING FACT...**
> The passage tomb on Knocknarea in Sligo is said to be the burial-place of the legendary Queen Maeve.

▼ ▶ *The huge burial mound at Newgrange, near Dublin, was built around 3100BC. A long, narrow passage leads to a burial chamber deep inside the mound. Above the entrance is an unusual 'roof-box' – a special slot through which the midwinter sun shines into the chamber.*

Every year, at exactly 8.58 am on December 21st (the winter solstice), the rising sun shines through this roof-box and right down the passage to light up the burial chamber

One of Newgrange's most distinctive features is the elaborate ornamentation – especially the carved spirals, which had a ritual significance

137

Julius Caesar

- **Julius Caesar** (*c.*100-44BC) was Rome's most famous general and leader. He was also a great speaker who had the power to excite huge crowds.

- **Caesar's** individuality was clear from the start. At 17, he defied Sulla, the dictator of Rome and married Cornelia, the daughter of the rebel leader Cinna. Cornelia died when Caesar was about 30.

- **Caesar** began as a politician and made himself popular by spending his own money on public entertainments.

- **In 60BC,** he formed a powerful triumvirate (group of three people) with Crassus and Pompey, which dominated Rome.

- **In 58BC,** Caesar led a brilliantly organized campaign to conquer Gaul (now northern France), and also invaded Britain.

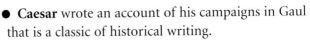

- **Caesar** wrote an account of his campaigns in Gaul that is a classic of historical writing.

- **Pompey** was alarmed by the fame that Caesar's conquests brought him. The two began a war that lasted five years, ending in Egypt in 48BC, where Caesar met and fell in love with Cleopatra.

- **By 45BC,** Caesar was undisputed master of the Roman Empire. The people elected him

▲ *Caesar was not only a brilliant general, but a great statesman who brought in many reforms and tried to stamp out corruption.*

dictator for life.

- **Caesar** was asked to become king, but he refused.

- **On March 15,** 44BC – called 'the Ides of March' – Caesar was stabbed to death as he entered the Senate. His assassins were a group led by Brutus and Cassius, who felt that his ambitions were a threat to Rome.

▶ *Caesar planned all kinds of bold economic, social and government reforms – but had been unable to carry many of them out by the time he was assassinated.*

The Guptas

- **The Guptas** were a family of rulers who reigned in northern India from AD320-c.500. This was one of India's golden ages, with writing, sculpture and other arts at their peak.

- **The Guptas** were originally a family of rich landowners, who took over control of the small kingdom of Magadha in the Ganges valley.

- **Chandragupta I** came to the throne in AD320. He extended his lands by marrying the right women.

- **Chandragupta's** son, Samudragupta, and his grandson, Chandragupta II, gained control over much of northern India by military conquests.

- **The Hindu** and Buddhist religions both began to develop and flourish during the great Gupta period.

- **Beautiful** temples and religious sculptures were created across northern India.

- **About AD450,** Kalidása, India's greatest poet and dramatist, wrote his famous play *Sákuntala*, filled with romance and adventure.

- **Music** and dance developed their highest classical form.

- **Hindu** mathematicians developed the decimal system (counting in tens) that we still use today.

- **Gupta** power collapsed by about AD500 under repeated attacks by Hun people from the north.

▶ *The Hindu and Buddhist sculpture and painting of the Gupta period has been the model for Indian art down the centuries.*

Gauls and Franks

- **The Gauls** were a Celtic people who lived in Western Europe, mainly in France.

- **The Gauls** could be brave warriors, and because the men had long hair and beards, the Romans thought them wild.

- **In 390BC,** Gauls crossed the Alps, swept down on Rome and sacked the city. They later withdrew, but they occupied northern Italy for almost 200 years.

- **In 278BC,** Gauls invaded what is now Turkey, settling the area called Galatia.

- **In the 50sBC,** Julius Caesar led a lightning Roman campaign to crush the Gauls. What is now France became Roman Gaul.

- **The Franks** were a German people split into two branches, the Salians and Ripurians.

- **In AD486,** Clovis, a king of the Salian Franks, invaded Roman Gaul to create a big kingdom covering modern France and Belgium.

... **FASCINATING FACT** ...
Franks were outnumbered 20 to 1
by Gallo-Romans – but France is
named after them.

◀ *Charles II of France, or Charles the Bald (AD823-877), fought many wars against his half brothers Louis the German and Lothair. In AD843 the Treaty of Verdun gave Charles the rule over the part of the empire which formed the basis for France.*

- **The first** period of Frankish rule in Gaul is called Merovingian (from AD486 to 751); the second is called Carolingian (751-987).

- **After Clovis's** death in 511, the Merovingian kingdom was divided and weakened. About 719, some Merovingian kings allowed a man called Charles Martel – *martel* means 'hammer' – to take control in the north as 'Mayor of the Palace'. Martel soon controlled the whole of Gaul.

▶ *In 52BC, the Gallic chief Vercingetorix led a last-ditch attempt to drive out the Romans. However, he was beaten, taken to Rome as Caesar's prize and executed.*

Early Africa

- **The world's first** known civilizations appeared in Africa along the Nile valley, in Egypt and further south in Nubia.

- **The first** Nubian civilization, called the A-group culture, appeared about 3200BC in the north of Nubia, known as Wawat. It was taken over by the Egyptians in 2950BC.

- **About 2000BC,** a new Nubian culture emerged in the then-fertile south, called Kush. Unlike the Wawat Nubians, who were Asian, the Kushites were black Africans.

- **Egypt** conquered Kush in 1500BC, but the Kushites, led by King Shabaka, conquered Egypt in 715BC. For 50 years, the Kushites were pharaohs and their capital, Napata, was seen as the centre of the ancient world.

- **In 666BC,** Assyrians drove the Kushites out of Egypt. However, the Kushites had learned iron-making from the Assyrians.

- **Napata** had iron-ore, but little wood for smelting the ore. So the Kushites moved their capital to Meroe – where they built great palaces, temples, baths and pyramids.

- **From Kush,** iron-making spread west, to Nigeria.

- **From AD100,** the city of Axum – now in northern Ethiopia – grew rich and powerful on ivory. About AD350, the Axumite king Aezanas invaded and overthrew Kush.

- **Kings** of Axum (later Ethiopia) were said to be descended from Jewish King Solomon and the Queen of Sheba. The Sheba were an Arab people who had settled in Axum.

- **King** Aezanas was converted to Christianity, but for 1500 years Axum/Ethiopia was Africa's only Christian country.

144

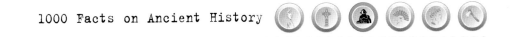

▲ *Africa was the birthplace of humanity, and rock paintings dating back 30,000 years are found all over Africa.*

145

Celts

- **Celts are** an ancient group of peoples who first appeared in the Danube valley in Germany about 3300 years ago.

- **The first** Celts are known as the Urnfield culture, because they put their cremated dead in urns.

▲ *Created in the early 800s AD, in Iona and Ireland, the Book of Kells is one of the great treasures of Celtic art.*

- **From 800** to 400BC, Celts spread across northern Europe. They took over modern-day France as people called Gauls, England as Britons and Ireland as Gaels.

- **The first** wave of expansion is called Halstatt culture. With bronze, Celts developed supreme metal-working skills.

- *c.*500BC, Celts learned to make iron and came into contact with Greeks and Etruscans. The 'La Tene' culture emerged.

- **In La Tene,** the distinctive Celtic swirls and spiral decoration appeared on weapons and ornaments.

- **After** Gauls sacked Rome, in 390BC, it seemed Celts might over-run Europe. But they were split into many tribes, and from 200BC they were pushed ever further west.

- **Some** early Celts used Greek letters to write in their own language, but our knowledge of them comes mostly from Greek and Roman authors.

- **Celts were** fierce warriors who charged into battle shouting, naked and stained with blue woad dye. But they valued poets higher than warriors. Their poets' tales of heroes and magic tell us how rich their culture was.

- **Celtic** clan society was highly organized and revolved around the chief of a clan, who made all the laws.

▶ *To face a Celtic warrior was a terrifying experience. Their bodies tattooed with blue dye (woad), they would let out bloodcurdling battle cries as they charged into combat.*

147

The first Britons

- **Britain** has been inhabited by human-like creatures for over 500,000 years. The oldest known settlement, at Star Carr in Yorkshire, dates back 10,000 years.

- **About 6-7000** years ago, Neolithic farmers arrived from Europe. They began to clear the island's thick woods to grow crops and build houses in stone.

- **The early** farmers created round monuments of stones and wooden posts called *henges*. The most famous is Stonehenge in Wiltshire.

- *c.*2300BC, new people from the Rhine arrived. They are called Beakerfolk, after their beaker-shaped pottery cups. They were Britain's first metal-workers.

- **Legend** has it that the name Britain came from Brutus, one of the sons of Aeneas, who fled from Troy.

- *c.*700BC, Celts arrived, often living in hillforts.

- **Iron axes** and ploughs enabled huge areas to be cleared and farmed, and the population rose.

- **When** Julius Caesar invaded, in 55 and 54BC, the Celtic people of England, called Britons, were divided into scores of tribes, such as the Catuvellauni and Atrebates.

- **Resistance** from tribal leaders such as Caratacus meant it took the Romans over a century to conquer the Britons.

- **The last** revolt was that of Queen Boudicca, in AD60.

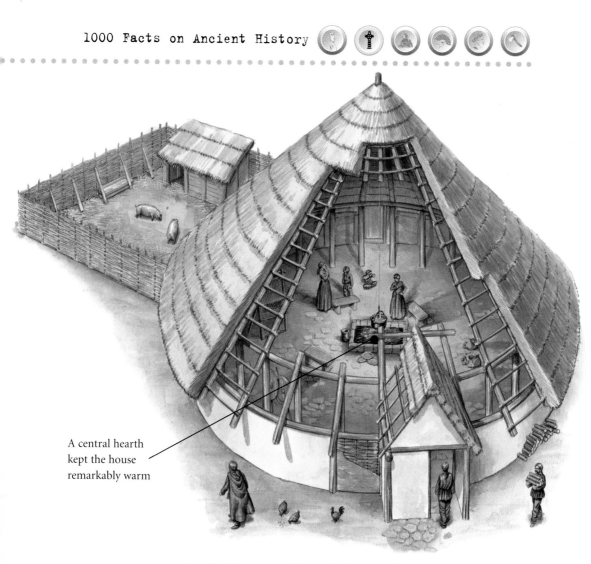

A central hearth
kept the house
remarkably warm

▲ *People of Bronze Age Britain lived in round houses like this,*
with thick stone walls and a steeply-pitched, thatched roof.

The fall of Rome

- **After the** death of Marcus Aurelius, in AD180, Rome was plagued by various serious political struggles.

- **The Praetorian** Guard (the emperor's personal soldiers) chose or deposed emperors at will, and there were 60 emperors between AD235 and 284 alone.

- **The Empire** fell into anarchy and was beset by famine, plague and invasion.

▼ *After the emperor Constantine moved his capital there in AD330, Byzantium (now Istanbul in Turkey) became the main defender of Roman civilization.*

- **Diocletian** (emperor from AD284) tried to make the empire easier to govern by splitting it in two halves – East and West. He asked Maximian to rule the west.

- **Diocletian** retired 'to grow cabbages' at his palace in Dalmatia, and soldiers tried to choose a new emperor.

- **Constantine,** commander of the Roman armies in Britain, defeated his rivals to become emperor. It is said that before the main battle, he saw a Christian cross in the sky. After his victory, he became Christian.

- **In BC330,** Constantine made Byzantium (now Istanbul) his capital and called it Constantinople.

- **After** Constantine's death, the empire fell into chaos again. It became split permanently into East and West.

- **The Western** empire suffered attacks from barbarians. Vandals invaded Spain and North Africa. Goths and Huns such as Attila attacked from the North.

- **In AD410,** Visigoths led by Alaric invaded Italy and sacked (burned and looted) Rome. In AD455, Vandals sacked Rome again. In AD476, the Western empire finally collapsed.

▶ *This coin was minted during the reign of Constantine. The inscription translates as 'Constantine, dutiful and wise ruler'.*

151

Early Christians

- **The first** Christians were Jews in Palestine, but followers like Paul soon spread the faith to gentiles (non-Jews) and countries beyond Palestine.

- **At first,** Roman rulers tolerated Christians, but after AD64, they saw Christians as a threat and persecuted them.

- **Persecution** strengthened Christianity by creating martyrs such as St Alban.

- **In AD313,** Emperor Constantine gave Christians freedom of worship and called the first great ecumenical (general) church council in 325.

- **By 392,** Christianity was the official religion of the empire.

- **When** the Roman Empire split into East and West, so too did Christianity, with the West focused on Rome and the East on Constantinople.

- **The head** of the Western church was the pope; the head of the Eastern church was called the patriarch. The first pope was Jesus's apostle St Peter, and there has been an unbroken line of popes ever since. But the power of the popes really began with St Gregory, in 590.

- **To separate** themselves from the official religion, some Christians, such as St Benedict, began to live apart as monks in monasteries.

- **After AD500,** monks spread Christianity over northwestern Europe.

- **Monasteries** became the main havens for learning in the West in the Dark Ages, which followed the fall of Rome.

▶ *Early Christian texts were manuscripts (hand-written) and monks spent years illuminating (decorating) them. The illuminated manuscripts of this time are among the most beautiful books ever made.*

152

IN NOMINE DÑI INCIPIT LIBER AUGUSTINI EPI DE CIVITATE
DEI MIRIFICE DISPUTATUS CONTRA PAGANOS ET DEOS.
EORUM DEMONES

GLORIOSISSI
MAM CIVITATEM DEI

MARCEL

S
I
V
E
IN.
HOC
TEM
PORVM
CVRSV

m inter impios peregrinatur ex fide uiuens. siue in illa stabilitate sedis
ernę quam nunc expectat per pacientiam quoadusq' iusticia conuer
t in iudiciũ deinceps adeptura per excellentē uictoriã ultimã & pace

Byzantine Empire

- **When** Rome collapsed, in AD476, Constantinople (now Istanbul in Turkey) became the capital of what historians call the Byzantine Empire. It became the centre of Western civilization for the next thousand years.

- **In the six** years after Constantine made Constantinople his capital, builders, architects and artists created one of the world's most magnificent cities.

- **Constantinople** was at the focus of trade routes between Asia and Europe. Silks, gems and ivories were traded for gold, grain, olives and wine. By charging 10% on all goods coming in and out, the city became fabulously rich.

- **When the** great emperor Justinian I came to the throne in 527, he tried to rebuild the Roman Empire. His general, Belisarius, reconquered Italy, and by 565 the Byzantine Empire stretched right round the Mediterranean.

- **Justinian** also built hundreds of churches, including the famous Hagia Sophia.

- **Justinian** modernized Roman law to create the basis of all Western legal systems. This is called the Code of Justinian.

- **The Byzantine** Empire was under constant attack – from Goths, Huns, Persians, Avars, Bulgars, Slavs, Vikings, Arabs, Berbers, Turks, Crusaders and Normans. But it repelled attackers, often with its secret weapon, 'Greek fire', invented in 650. This was a mix of quick-lime, petrol and sulphur, which burst into flames when it hit water.

▶ *Justinian I was the greatest Byzantine emperor, although his general's secretary, Procopius, described him as 'a demon incarnate'. He ruled with his beautiful former actress wife, Theodora. Justinian relied on her for support and advice, and it was she who changed laws to improve the lives of women and the poor.*

- **In 1204,** Constantinople was ransacked by Crusader knights who were short of money. Almost every treasure in the city was stolen and it never recovered from this devastating blow. The city's population dwindled from 1 million to just 60,000 over the next 200 years.

- **Constantinople** was finally conquered by the Turkish Sultan Mehmet II in 1453.

...**FASCINATING FACT**...
29 of Byzantium's 88 emperors died violent deaths, and the endless conspiracies at court have given us the word 'Byzantine' for dark intrigues.

▼ *At its height, Constantinople was graced by some of the ancient world's most magnificent buildings. This picture shows the tranquil palace quarter. The rest of the city was noisy and crowded.*

The Hippodrome was based on the Circus Maximus in Rome

60,000 spectators watched chariot races here

The Hagia Sophia, now a museum, is the world's oldest Christian cathedral

Sui, Tang and Song

- In AD581, Yang Chien seized the throne in the north of China and in so doing founded the Sui dynasty.

- **Yang Chien** conquered the south and reunited China for the first time since the fall of the Han in AD220.

- **Under** the second Sui emperor, Yang Di, China's Grand Canal was rebuilt on a huge scale, linking China's main rivers. Other canals extended the network.

- **Yang Di was** betrayed by one of his 3000 mistresses and was strangled in AD618. Li Yuan, an ambitious Sui minister, then seized the throne to found the Tang dynasty.

- **Under** the Tang trade grew, China became rich again and the arts and sciences flourished.

- **By AD751, China** was the world's largest empire and the capital, Chang'an, was the world's largest city, with over 1 million inhabitants.

- **Chinese** people were the first to drink tea and sit on chairs.

- **Poets** such as Li Po (AD701-762) wrote of his love of wild mountains and the fleeting nature of happiness. China's tradition of great landscape painting began and one of the earliest printed books, *The Diamond Sutra*, was made in AD868.

- **By AD800,** the Tang dynasty was beginning to break up, Chang'an declined and China descended into turmoil.

- **Order** was restored in AD960, when the Song family began to rule from the city of Kaifeng. The Song lasted until AD1276, when the Mongol Kublai Khan conquered China.

▶ *Gunpowder was invented in the Tang era. The Chinese used it first to make fabulous fireworks and later weapons.*

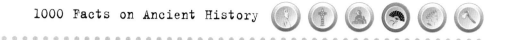

Barbarians

- **Barbarians** is what the Romans called all the peoples living outside the empire, who they thought of as uncivilized.

- **Barbarian** people rarely lived in large towns. Instead they lived in forts or small farming villages.

- **Many** were brave warriors but many too were skilled craftsmen, poets and humble farmers.

- **The Romans** thought barbarians wild and crude, but they survived and built a lasting civilization as the peoples of northern and western Europe.

- **They** seemed ill-disciplined in battle to the Romans. They rode horses and appeared in vast, wild, terrifying hordes.

- **The Goths** were German peoples who overran the western Roman empire in the 4th and 5th centuries AD. They were divided into Ostrogoths in the east, near the Black Sea, and Visigoths on the Danube. It was the Visigoths who, under their king Alaric, finally broke Rome in AD476.

- **Italians** later used the term 'gothic' to sneer at what they saw as the ugly cathedrals of northern Europe and the term stuck.

- **The Vandals** were a German tribe who arrived in Europe from the east in the 1st century BC. When driven west by the Huns in c.AD380, they took over Spain and North Africa.

- **Vandals** swept down through Italy in AD455 to sack Rome and gave us the current word 'vandal' for destructive troublemakers.

- **The Huns** were nomadic Mongols from eastern Asia who arrived in Europe *c.*AD370, driving everyone before them, until finally defeated in AD455. The Huns were bogeymen for Romans. One Roman said, 'They have a sort of shapeless lump, not a face, and pinholes for eyes' – perhaps because Huns bandaged children's skulls to deform as they grew. The most feared Hun was Attila.

▶ *Alaric was the great Gothic leader who took Rome in 410. He looted the city but spared the churches. Alaric planned to settle in Africa, but a storm forced him to stop at Cozenza in southern Italy, where he died.*

159

Roman Britain

- **The Roman** occupation began in earnest when the armies of Claudius landed at Richborough in Kent in AD43. All of England and Wales was conquered by AD78.

- **Scotland** remained beyond Roman control. In AD122-130, the 118-km-long stone wall that is now called Hadrian's wall was built right across the country to act as a frontier.

- **The Roman** army in Britain was powerful. There were three legions (5000 men each) at York, Chester and Caerleon, plus 40,000 auxiliaries.

- **Roman** Britain was ruled by a Roman governor, but the Romans co-opted local chiefs to help.

- **The Romans** built the first proper towns in Britain – like St Albans, Gloucester and Lincoln – with typical Roman features such as baths and theatres.

- **Demand** for food and leather from the army and the new towns boosted farming. Large estates centred on Roman-style villas grew rich, but even small farmers did well.

- **Most people** were bilingual, speaking both Celtic and Latin, and many adopted Roman lifestyles.

▶ *King Arthur became the greatest hero in British legend, but the real Arthur was probably a British chief who, for a while, turned the tide against the Anglo-Saxons with a victory at Mt Badon around AD530-550.*

160

- **When barbarians** attacked the empire on the continent in the AD300s, leading generals from Italy were sent to reorganise defences. Power fell into the hands of tyrants like the British king Vortigern (AD425-250).

- **Vortigern** invited Anglo-Saxons from Germany to settle in the east to help him against rebel Britons. But the Anglo-Saxons soon turned against him and invited in others of their kind to join them.

- **Villas and** towns were abandoned and Britons fled west or abroad as the Anglo-Saxons moved in.

▲ *Hadrian's wall may have acted as a defence, keeping 'barbarians' out of Roman territory. It is generally accepted that the emperor Hadrian wanted to mark the northern boundary of his empire. The wall itself took six years to build, and was modified for many years after.*

161

Muhammed

- **Muhammed** (c.AD570-632) was the Arab prophet whose teachings form the basis of the Islamic religion.

- **Muslims** (followers of Islam) believe Muhammed was the last and greatest prophet of God, who they called Allah.

- **Muhammed** was born in Mecca in Arabia.

- **His father** died before he was born and his mother died when he was a child. He was brought up by his grandfather and uncle, tending sheep and camels.

- **At the age** of 25, Muhammed entered the service of a rich widow of 40 called Khadjia and later married her. They had two sons and four daughters.

- **When** he was 35, Muhammed was asked to restore a sacred stone damaged in a flood. He had a vision that told him to become a prophet and proclaim the word of God.

▼ *Each year, thousands of Muslims from all over the world flock to the Ka'ba shrine at Mecca, in modern Saudi Arabia.*

162

◀ *The Qu'ran is Islam's holy book of Muhammed's teachings.*

- **The people** of Mecca resented Muhammed's preaching, and in AD622 he emigrated to Medina, in Saudi Arabia.

- **In Medina,** he attracted many followers. The Meccans went to war against Medina, but were driven back.

- **In AD630,** Muhammed re-entered Mecca in triumph, pardoned the people and set up a mosque there.

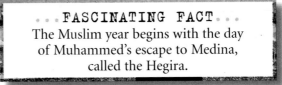

... FASCINATING FACT ...
The Muslim year begins with the day
of Muhammed's escape to Medina,
called the Hegira.

163

What people wore

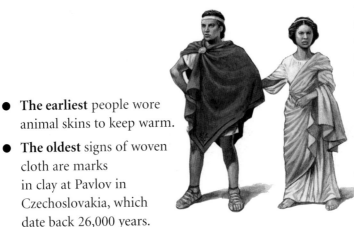

- **The earliest** people wore animal skins to keep warm.

- **The oldest** signs of woven cloth are marks in clay at Pavlov in Czechoslovakia, which date back 26,000 years.

◄ Greek clothes were very simple – essentially pieces of wool or linen wrapped round to make a tunic, dress or cloak. Young men typically wore a short cloak (chlamys) over a tunic sewn up at the side and fastened at the shoulder. Women wore a dress (chiton) made from a rectangle of cloth. They wore a longer cloak called a himation.

- **Most of** our knowledge of ancient costumes comes from vases, statues and wall paintings. Colours have often faded, but we know from paintings such as those in the Roman city of Pompeii, preserved under volcanic ash, that ancient clothes were often colourful.

◄ Egyptians wore clothes made mainly of white linen. At first, men wore a short kilt, but later they wore long, wrap-around skirts. Egyptian women at first wore sheath-like dresses. After 1500BC, men and women both wore loose robes like these, made from rectangles of cloth.

- **The oldest** surviving clothes come from 5000-year-old Egyptian tombs.

- **The deep** blue dye indigo, from the indigo plant, has been found in Egyptian cloth from 4400 years ago.

- **Tyrian** purple was a purple dye, much-prized in ancient times. It came from Tyre (modern Lebanon) and was made from Purpura and Murex snails.

- **People** such as the ancient Egyptians often wore simple sandals or shoes of papyrus or leather. But the Greek dramatist Aeschylus is said to have invented the platform shoe.

- **Minoan** women of 3500 years ago, unusually for ancient times, wore tight-waisted dresses. Their breasts were left exposed.

- **Ordinary** Roman citizens wore an unbleached white toga. Coloured borders showed a particular status. Public officials at functions had togas with purple borders, called a *toga praetexta*. Early Roman generals wore togas dyed in Tyrian purple. From the time of Augustus, only the emperor wore a purple toga.

▲ In the north of Europe, Celtic peoples wore warm clothes made mainly of dyed wool and leather. Women wore thick dresses and headscarfs. Men wore long tunics, leggings and a cloak.

◀ Roman clothing was quite similar to the Greeks'. Men and women wore tunics, called stola (women) or tunica (men). Citizens of Rome were allowed to wear a carefully draped cloth called a toga over their tunic.

165

Monastery life

- **In religions** like Christianity and Buddhism, some devout people step out of ordinary life and live in a monastery, a community devoted entirely to religion.

- **The earliest** Christian monastery was that of the hermit St Anthony of Thebes, who went to live in the Egyptian desert about AD271, and attracted loyal followers.

- **Basil the Great** (*c.*AD329-379) and his sister Macrina the Younger founded monasteries for men and women on their estate in Cappadocia in Turkey.

▲ *British and Irish monks laboured to create beautiful illustrated books by hand. This is the* Lindisfarne Gospel.

- **Monasticism** spread rapidly throughout the Byzantine Empire between the 4th and 7th centuries AD.

- **In the West,** monasticism grew more slowly, so St Martin of Tours (AD316-397) sent out monks to start new communities. They were very successful in Britain and Ireland.

- **Monasteries** such as Lindisfarne and Malmesbury were centres of learning in the Dark Ages.

- **The most** famous scholar-monk was St Bede of (*c.*AD672-735), known for his history of the English people.

- **The most** famous British monastery was the Scottish Isle of Iona, set up by St Columba in AD563.

- **St Benedict** (*c.*AD480-547) developed a particular way of living for monks at Monte Cassino in Italy. By 1000, most monasteries followed Benedictine rules.

- **Monasteries** were very vulnerable to Viking raids. Monks were often killed and many treasures lost, and so the monastic life lost some of its attraction.

▶ *Before the days of mass-printing, monks hand-copied texts because they needed books for their studies.*

The spread of Islam

- **Muslims** believe that their religion began the day a prophet named Mohammed left Mecca in AD622, but it was after his death in 632 that it really began to grow.

- **The spread** of Islam was led by *caliphs* (which means 'successors').

- **Islam** expanded by conquest, and many peoples only became Muslims after they were conquered. But Muslim conquerors were tolerant of other religions.

- **The Muslims** regarded a conquest as a *jihad* (holy war) and this gave them a powerful zeal.

- **The Muslim** Arabs conquered Iraq (AD637), Syria (AD640), Egypt (AD641) and Persia (AD650).

▼ *Five times every day, devout Muslims the world over face the holy city of Mecca to pray.*

- **By AD661**, the great Islamic Empire stretched from Tunisia to India. Its capital was at Damascus.

- **The first** Muslims were Arabs, and as Islam spread, so did Arabs, but the empire contained many peoples.

- **Mohammed** commanded men to 'seek knowledge, even as far as China'. Many Muslims became great scholars.

- **Arts and** sciences flourished under Islam to make it one of the most cultured, advanced societies in the world.

▼ *The Dome of the Rock in Jerusalem, built by Abd al-Malik, was one of the first of many beautiful buildings created by Muslims.*

The Fujiwaras

- **The Fujiwaras** were the family who dominated Japan for five centuries from the 7th century AD.

- **The Fujiwaras'** power really began in 858, when Fujiwara Yoshifusa married the old emperor. When he died, Yoshifusa became regent to their young son.

- **The Fujiwaras** kept their position by marrying more daughters to emperors, and creating the role of an all-powerful *kampaku* (chancellor).

- **The Fujiwara** kampaku or regent ran the country while the emperor dealt with religious matters.

- **Fujiwara** power peaked with Michinaga (966-1028).

- **Michinaga's** mansions were more splendid than palaces and filled with banquets, concerts, poetry and picnics.

- **Many women** were novelists and poets, and love affairs were conducted via cleverly poetic letters.

- **The brilliant** court life of Michinaga was captured in the famous novel *The Tale of Genji* by the lady Murasaki.

- **During** Michinaga's reign, warrior families gained the upper hand by quelling rural rebellions, so bringing about the Fujiwaras' downfall.

▶ *The* Tales of Genji *is thought to be the world's oldest full-length novel. It was written about AD1000 by Murasaki Shikibu, a lady-in-waiting to the empress of Japan. It tells the story of Prince Genji and his various loves.*

.... FASCINATING FACT ....
Sei Shonagon, a lady at Michinaga's court, wrote a famous *Pillow Book* – a diary about what she saw.

171

Anglo-Saxons

- **The Angles**, Saxons and Jutes were peoples from Denmark and Germany who invaded Britain and settled there between AD450 and 600.

- **The Britons** resisted at first, but by 650 they were driven back into the west or made slaves.

- **The Angles** settled in East Anglia and the Midlands, the Saxons in Sussex, Essex and Wessex (Dorset and Hampshire).

- **Each tribe** had its own kingdom, yet by 700 most people in the south thought of themselves as English.

- **Seven** leading kingdoms formed a 'heptarchy': Essex, Kent, Sussex, Wessex, East Anglia, Mercia and Northumbria.

- **One king** was *bretwalda* (overlord), but the kingdoms vied for power.

- **When Ethelbert** of Kent was bretwalda, in 597, St Augustine converted him to Christianity. Christianity spread rapidly throughout England. English monasteries became the universities of Europe. Masons from Gaul and Rome built stone churches.

- **Most** Anglo-Saxons were farmers. Others were warriors, as their famous epic poem of heroism, *Beowulf*, shows.

▲ *In 1939, the burial ship of the overlord Raedwald (died 625) was discovered at Sutton Hoo in East Anglia. This helmet is one of the treasures it held.*

172

- **In the 700s,** Danish raiders conquered all of England but Wessex. They were pushed back by King Alfred, but attacks resumed in the reign of Ethelred II (978-1016).

- **The last** Anglo-Saxon king was Ethelred II's son, Edward the Confessor (1042-1066).

▶ *The Scandinavian Vikings who made continual raids on Britain were descended from earlier 'barbarian' peoples.*

◀ *Anglo-Saxon villages were made from materials such as wood, thatch and wattle (woven branches).*

173

Bulgars

- **The Bulgars** were an Asian people who arrived in Europe – on the Volga River – around AD370.

- **The Bulgars** were skilled horse-warriors. They were ruled by *khans* (chiefs) and *boyars* (noblemen).

- **The Bulgars** attacked the fringes of the Byzantine Empire until they were in turn attacked by another Asian people called the Avars.

- **After Kurt** became the Bulgar Khan in 605, the Bulgars re-established themselves on the steppes, but when Kurt died, the Bulgars split into five hordes, or groups.

- **Four of** the five Bulgar hordes vanished from history, but the fifth was led by Asparukh Khan, west into the Danube valley. Here they overpowered the Slavs living there to create a Bulgarian Empire.

- **Bulgarian** Khans were called *caesars* or *czars* after helping Byzantine emperor Justinian II in 710.

- **The Bulgars** were more often at odds with the Byzantines. They were usually beaten, but after one victory, Krum Khan (803-814) lined Byzantine emperor Nicephorus's skull with silver to make a drinking cup.

- **The Byzantines** sent St Cyril and his brother St Methodius to convert the Bulgar people to Christianity. They succeeded when Czar Boris I was baptized in 864.

- **St Cyril** invented the Cyrillic alphabet, still used by Russians and other eastern Europeans today.

- **The Bulgarian** empire peaked under Simeon I (893-927). Its capital, Preslav, imitated Constantinople in splendour.

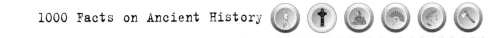

▲ *In the 800s, the Bulgars were converted to Christianity and adopted the Eastern Orthodox Church of the Byzantines. They began to create icons (religious images) like this.*

175

The caliphs

- **The caliphs** were the rulers of Islam. The word *caliph* means 'successor', and they were all meant to be successors of Muhammed after he died in ad632.

- **The first** caliph was Muhammed's father-in-law, Abu Bakr. After that came Umar, Uthman and Ali.

- **The first** four caliphs are called the Rashidun ('rightly guided') because they were the only caliphs accepted by everyone.

- **When Ali** died, in 661, Islam was torn apart by civil war. Some Muslims, called Shi'ites, saw only Ali's successors, the *imams*, as leaders. Most Muslims followed the Umayyad family, who became caliphs in Damascus.

- **The 14 Umayyad** caliphs expanded the Islamic empire by conquest through North Africa and into Spain. But it proved too much for them to handle.

- **In 750,** the last of the Umayyad caliphs – Marwan II – was beaten at the Battle of the Great Zab by the rival Abbasids, who were descended from Muhammed's uncle.

- **The 38** Abbasid caliphs turned their eyes eastwards and made a new capital at Baghdad, which soon became the richest city in the world.

- **Under the** Abbasids, Islam became famous for its science, learning and art, especially during the time of Harun al-Rashid.

- **One Umayyad** escaped to set up a rival caliphate in Spain (756-1031).

- **Descendants** of Muhammed's daughter Fatimah became caliphs in Egypt, creating the great city of Cairo.

▶ *Under the Abbasid caliphs, Islamic artists made strikingly beautiful ceramic tiles and glassware.*

▼ *This mosque in Cairo, Egypt is dedicated to the caliph Ali, one of the original caliphs who who was accepted by all the people.*

Alfred the Great

▲ *This enamel and gold jewel was found near Athelney. It is inscribed with the words* Aelfred me ech eh t gewyrcan *– Old English for 'Alfred ordered me to be made'.*

- **Alfred the Great** (AD849-899) was the greatest of the Anglo-Saxon kings.

- **Alfred became** king of Wessex in 871, at a time when the Danes (Vikings) had overrun East Anglia, Northumbria and Mercia.

- **In 878,** a series of ferocious Danish attacks drove Alfred to hide on the isle of Athelney – in the Somerset marshes.

- **While on the run,** Alfred is said to have hidden in a pigherd's cottage. He was so tired he fell asleep by the fire, letting some cakes burn. Not realizing he was the king, the pigherd's wife scolded him.

- **From Athelney,** Alfred secretly assembled an army and emerged to score a decisive victory over the Danes at Edington. The Danes agreed to withdraw to East Anglia and their king Guthrum became a Christian.

- **In 886,** Alfred recaptured London and forced the Danes to stay within an area called Danelaw.

- **Alfred built** forts, reorganized his army and also created England's first navy to defend the country against invasions.

- **Alfred was** a wise and kindly king who created sound laws, protected the weak from corrupt judges and made laws to help the poor and needy.

● **Alfred was** a scholar who encouraged learning. He decreed that all young men should learn to read English, and made important books available in English.

...FASCINATING FACT...
Alfred translated many books from Latin into English so that his people could read them.

▶ Alfred encouraged the building of new ships. He realized that a strong fleet would help his navy defend against invasion.

The Berbers

- **The Berbers** were the people who lived in North Africa before various other peoples arrived.

- **'Berber'** comes from *barbara*, Roman for 'barbarians'.

- **Numidian** Berbers allied themselves with Carthage (in what is now Tunisia), the great city created when Phoenician traders from Lebanon settled there 3000 years ago.

- **The Berbers** coped with invasions from Carthaginians, and then Romans, Vandals and Byzantine people, by withdrawing south into the desert, living their lives as bands of marauders.

- **In the 7th century** AD, Islamic Arabs invaded North Africa and many Berbers became Muslims.

- **The Berbers** kept their independence by changing Islam to their own tastes. They based their religion around *marabouts*, holy men who lived very frugally and morally.

- **After 740,** Berbers regained control of North Africa from the Umayyad caliphs.

- **The Berbers** built empires extending into Spain under the Almohads (1121-1269) and Almoravids (1061-1145).

- **Ibn Tumart** was the first Almohad leader, from *c.*1121. He claimed to be the Mahdi, the holy man whose coming was predicted by Mohammed.

- **The Berber** empires fell to the Arabs in the 12th century.

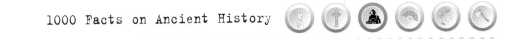

▲ *When their empires fell, the Berbers survived in the harsh conditions of the Sahara desert.*

The Vikings

- **The Vikings** were daring raiders from Norway, Sweden and Denmark. Between AD800 and 1100, they swept in on the coasts of northwest Europe in their longships, searching for rich plunder to carry away.

- **People** were terrified by the lightning raids of the Vikings. A prayer of the time went, 'Deliver us, O Lord, from the fury of the Norsemen (Vikings). They ravage our lands. They kill our women and children.'

- **Vikings** prided themselves on their bravery in battle. Most fought on foot with swords, spears and axes. Rich Vikings rode on horseback.

- **Shock troops** called *berserkers* led the attack. *Berserk* is Norse for 'bare shirt' as they wore no armour. Before a battle, they became fighting-mad through drink and drugs and trusted in their god Odin to keep them safe.

- **The word** 'Viking' was only used later. People of the time called them Norsemen. The word Viking probably came from Vik, a pirate centre in Norway. When Norsemen went 'a-viking', they meant fighting as a pirate. Swedish Vikings who settled in eastern Europe may have been called Rus, and so Russia was named after them.

- **Not all Vikings** were pirates. At home, they were farmers and fishermen, merchants and craftworkers. Many went with the raiders and settled in the north of France, in northern England and in Dublin.

- **The Vikings** attacked mainly Britain and Ireland, but raided as far as Gibraltar and into the Mediterranean.

- **In Eastern** Europe, the Vikings' ships carried them inland up various rivers. They ventured far through Russia and the Ukraine, sometimes marauding as far south as Constantinople, which they called 'Miklagard', the big city.

- **The Norsemen** who settled in northern
France were called Normans. The Norman
king, William the Conqueror, who invaded
England in 1066, was descended from their
leader, Rollo.

▶ A hammer like this one
was used at many stages in a
Viking's life – raised over the
newborn, laid in the bride's lap at
weddings, or carved on a grave.
The hammer was the symbol of
the great Viking god, Thor. Other
major Viking gods were Odin and
Frey. The Anglo-Saxons had the
same gods and their names have
given us some days of the week:
Odin's or Wodin's day
(Wednesday), Thor's day
(Thursday) and Frey's or Frigg's
day (Friday).

◀ At home, most Vikings were farmers.
The women were left in charge when their
husbands went raiding.

183

Viking voyages

- **The Vikings** were great seafarers who made some of the most remarkable voyages of ancient times.

- **The Vikings** sailed east through the Baltic Sea and up the Vistula and Dnieper Rivers.

- **The Vikings** sailed west around the British Isles, and south around Spain into the Mediterranean.

- **The most** daring Viking voyages were out across the then-unknown open ocean of the North Atlantic.

- **From AD900,** the Vikings sailed to, and settled on, remote islands to the far north – including Iceland, the Faroes and Greenland.

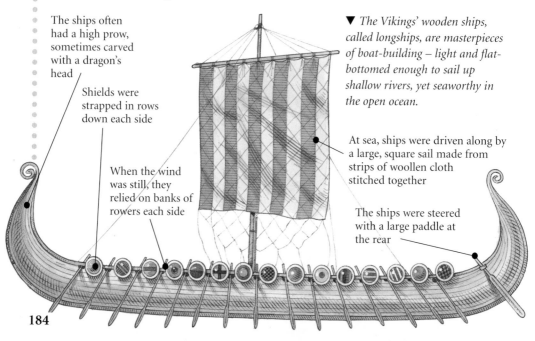

The ships often had a high prow, sometimes carved with a dragon's head

Shields were strapped in rows down each side

When the wind was still, they relied on banks of rowers each side

▼ *The Vikings' wooden ships, called longships, are masterpieces of boat-building – light and flat-bottomed enough to sail up shallow rivers, yet seaworthy in the open ocean.*

At sea, ships were driven along by a large, square sail made from strips of woollen cloth stitched together

The ships were steered with a large paddle at the rear

- **About 800,** Vikings led by Ohthere reached the remote Siberian islands of Novaya Zemlya in the Arctic.

- **In 1000,** Bjarni Herjulffson was blown off-course sailing home from Greenland and saw an unknown shore.

- **Leif Eriksson** sailed west to find this unknown shore. Stories called *Sagas* tell how he found a new land. The Vikings called it 'Vinland', because it was said to be abundant in 'wine berries'. The wine berries he found were probably cranberries.

- **Most experts** now think Vinland is North America, and Leif was the first European to reach it.

- **In AD1004,** the Viking Thorfinn took 130 people to settle in Vinland and stayed three years. Remains of Thorfinn's settlement were found in 1963, at L'Anse aux Meadows, on the northern tip of Newfoundland.

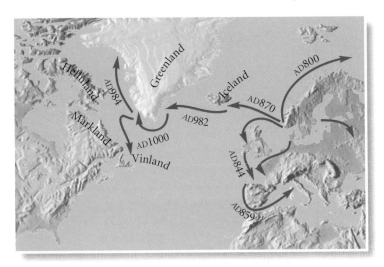

▶ *Viking weaponry included a spear, knife and protective shield. Vikings held their weapons sacred.*

◀ *This map shows just some of the remarkable voyages made by the Vikings, and their approximate dates. Names are the Viking names.*

185

Viking society

- **Vikings ate** beef, cheese, eggs and milk from their farms, meat from deer, elks and seals caught by hunters and fish such as cod, herring and salmon.

- **Vikings lived** in one-storey wooden houses with slanted roofs of turf or straw and no windows. At the centre was a hearth for warmth and cooking. The man of the house sat on a chair called the high seat; the rest of the family sat on benches.

- **Viking men** wore trousers and a long-sleeved smock shirt. Women wore long woollen or linen dresses.

- **Viking men** were allowed to have two or three wives, and marriages were arranged by parents.

- **A Viking woman,** unusually for the time, could own her own property and divorce her husband.

- **Skalds (Viking poets)** went into battle to report on them in verse.

- **The Vikings** were great storytellers. They told of their adventures in long stories called *Sagas*.

◀ *Viking god Odin was said to ride on an eight-legged horse called Sleipnir, accompanied by two ravens that brought him news of any battles.*

> **. . . FASCINATING FACT . . .**
> Viking villages were ruled by a council
> called the *Thing* or *Folkmoot*.

186

- **At first**, the Sagas were only spoken. From 1100 to 1300, they were written. The most famous is Njal's Saga.

- **Vikings were** very religious and had several gods. They believed if they died fighting they would go to Valhalla, a special hall in Asgard, the gods' home.

◀ *Viking women looked after the children and the home, but also had rights that were unusual for women at this time.*

187

The first Russians

- **Little is** known of the earliest days of Russia, because it was inhabited mainly by nomadic peoples who left few records – such as the Cimmerians (1200-700BC) and later Huns and Khazars.

- **In the 800s** AD, Russia was on the major trade route from northwestern Europe to the world's richest cities – Constantinople and Baghdad.

- **Slavic** peoples set up trading towns such as Novgorod. They traded in amber, furs, honey, wax and wood.

- **From around** 860, Viking adventurers raided and traded in the region. They were known as the Varangian Rus. The most famous of them was Rurik of Jutland, who took over Novgorod.

- **The city** of Kiev grew up further south, on the Dnieper River.

- **Soon** the Varangian 'grand prince' of Kiev ruled over a vast area historians call Kievan Rus. This covered what is now the Ukraine and eastern Russia.

- **Around 970,** the Slavs took over Kiev – under Prince Svyatoslav and his son, Vladimir.

- **Vladimir** made Kievan Rus the first Russian nation.

- **Legend** says that Vladimir sent people far and wide to study different religions. Nothing impressed them until they reached the Hagia Sophia in Constantinople. They were so stunned 'they knew not whether they were in heaven or on earth'.

- **Kiev** quickly adopted Byzantine Christianity. Within 50 years it had 200 beautiful churches – including its own Hagia Sophia – and Vladimir was Russia's first saint.

▶ *The beautiful cathedral of St. Sophia in the city of Kiev resembles the Hagia Sophia in old Constantinople.*

Harun al-Rashid

- **Harun al-Rashid** (766-809) was the most famous of all the caliphs.

- **In Harun's time,** Baghdad became the most glamorous city in the world, famed for its luxury as well as its poetry, music and learning.

- **Harun** was famous far and wide. He sent ambassadors to the Chinese emperor and an elephant to Charlemagne.

- **Harun's wife**, Zubaydah, would only drink from silver and gold cups studded with gems.

- **Harun** was a great patron of the arts, and gave lavish gifts to poets and musicians. Yet he also enjoyed watching dogs fight – and often had people executed.

- **Stories** tell how Harun would wander in the moonlight with his friend Abu Nuwas, the brilliant poet, as well as Masrur the executioner.

- **Harun** has become famous because he features in the famous collection of 200-odd tales of *The Thousand and One Nights*, or *The Arabian Nights*.

- *The Arabian Nights* includes such famous characters as Aladdin and his genie, Ali Baba and Sinbad the Sailor.

- **The tales** begin with King Shahriyar of Samarkand distraught by his wife's unfaithfulness. He vows to marry a new girl each night and behead her in the morning.

- **The lovely** princess Scheherazade insists on marrying the king, then at night tells him a tale so entertaining that he lets her live another day to finish it. One story leads to another for 1001 nights, by which time the king has fallen completely in love with her.

◄ *The magic and romance of Harun's Baghdad is captured in the tales of* The Arabian Nights.

Holy Roman Empire

- **The Holy Roman** Empire was a mostly German empire, which lasted from 800 until 1806.

- **It began** when Pope Leo III tried to gain the protection of Charlemagne, the King of the Franks, by reviving the idea of the Roman Empire.

- **Pope Leo III** is said to have taken Charlemagne by surprise in St Peter's church in Rome – on Christmas Day 800 – and to have placed the crown of the empire on his head.

- **Charlemagne's** Frankish Empire, including France, Germany and Italy, became the Holy Roman Empire.

- **When Charlemagne** died, in 814, the new Holy Roman Empire fell apart.

- **150 years later,** in 962, the German king, Otto I, gained control of Italy as well as Germany and insisted the pope crown him Holy Roman Emperor.

- **Over the** centuries, the empire was continually beset by conflicts with both powerful Germans and the pope.

- **In 1076,** Pope Gregory VII and Emperor Henry IV were vying for control. Henry's subjects sided with the pope, so Henry had to give way.

- **Gregory** forced Henry to stand barefoot in snow for three days outside his castle in Tuscany to beg for a pardon.

- **The pope's** Vatican and other Italian cities gained almost complete independence from the emperor.

▲ *In 1250 the Holy Roman Empire extended from the North to the Mediterranean Sea. This is highlighted in brown. The Papal states (yellow), separated the Kingdom of the Two Scicilies, which also belonged to the Emperor.*

The Toltecs

- **By 900,** the city of Teotihuacán was destroyed and much of Mexico was in the hands of warrior tribes from the north.

- **Legend** says that Teotihuacán was destroyed by one of these warrior tribes called the Toltecs, led by their ruler Mixcóatl. The name Mixcóatl means 'Cloud Serpent'.

- **Under Mixcóatl's son,** Topiltzin, the Toltec were said to have built an empire and a capital at Tollan, now thought to be Tula, 45 km north of Mexico City.

- **Topiltzin** introduced the cult of the god Quetzalcóatl ('Feathered Serpent'), and took the name himself.

> **···FASCINATING FACT···**
> The name *Toltec* has many meanings: 'cultured person', 'city-type' and 'reed people'.

- **The Toltecs** were not only great warriors but fine builders and craftsmen. Tollan was full of pyramids, temples and other huge, impressive buildings.

- **Legend** says Topiltzin Quetzalcóatl was driven out of Tollan by jealous rivals – including the priests of the god Tezcatlipoca ('Smoking Mirror').

- **After leaving** Tollan, Quetzalcóatl sailed east into the Gulf of Mexico, vowing to return one day.

- **The Aztecs** were greatly influenced by the Toltecs. The Aztecs got the idea of human sacrifices from the priests of Tezcatlipoca. Some Aztecs believed that, when the Spanish arrived in 1519, it was Quetzalcóatl returning in vengeance.

- **The Toltec** empire broke up in the 12th century and Tollan vanished.

▶ *Toltec temples in Tollan were guarded by stone statues of warriors such as this.*

The Maoris

- **No human** set foot on New Zealand before around 2000 years ago.

- **The first settlers** in New Zealand were Polynesians.

- **The early** Polynesian settlers came to New Zealand by canoe, from islands in the Pacific.

- **In c.AD100,** Polynesians called the Morioris came here to settle from the Cook, Marquesas or Society Islands.

- **Maori tradition** tells how the Maoris arrived in waves of migration, beginning about 1150 and ending with the coming of a great fleet from the mythical land of Hawaiki, 200 years later.

- **Hawaiki** is thought to be the Pacific island of Tahiti.

▲ *The Maoris lived mostly near the coast or by rivers and travelled in light, swift canoes.*

- **Archaeologists** have found signs of Maori settlement in New Zealand dating back to AD800 and earlier.

- **The first Maoris** lived mainly by hunting and fishing.

- **Maoris were** skilled woodworkers, building beautiful wooden houses covered in carvings.

▶ *The beautiful island of Tahiti is a tropical paradise. It is is said to be the mythical land of Hawaiki, from which fleets of Maori settlers sailed.*

197

Charlemagne

- **In AD732,** the Frankish (early French) leader Charles Martel halted the great Muslim invasion of Europe – in battle at Tours in central France.

- **Charles Martel's son,** Pepin the Short, made sure of his family's hold on power in the Frankish kingdom. In 768, Pepin's son Charlemagne became 'King of the Franks'.

- **Charlemagne** (742-814) was the greatest European ruler for 1000 years after the fall of Rome.

- **Charlemagne's** name means 'Charles the Great'.

- **Charlemagne** was a great military leader, taking his armies on 53 successful campaigns. He scored victories against the Moors in Spain, and against Saxons and Avars in central Europe.

- **By 796,** Charlemagne had created an empire joining France, Germany, northern Italy and northern Spain.

- **Charlemagne** was a Christian, and in AD800, the pope made Charlemagne Holy Roman Emperor.

- **Charlemagne** was a great ruler who set up an effective law system and introduced the idea of juries in trials.

- **Charlemagne** knew Latin, German and Greek and encouraged scholarship, helped by the great teacher Alcuin.

- **The palace** school in Charlemagne's capital, Aachen, was the most important school in Europe.

▶ *This beautiful goblet, known as 'Charlemagne's cup' dates back to Crusader times.*

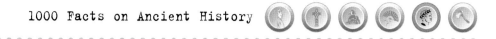
▼ *After his death, many legends grew up about Charlemagne. We know that he must have been a powerful personality. One eyewitness said: 'He had a broad and strong body of unusual height…and strode with a firm step and held himself like a man.'*

The Magyars

- **The plains** by the river Danube (an area now in Hungary) were settled early in the history of humankind, although little is known of the region before it formed the Roman provinces Dacia and Pannonia. At this time, it was home to Celts and Slavs.

- **Roman Dacia** and Pannonia fell early to the barbarian invaders – Goths, Huns and Avars.

- **In 796,** the Avars were crushed by Charlemagne.

- **In 892,** another Frankish king called Arnulf asked a people called the Magyars to help him against the Moravians, who now lived on the Danube plain.

- **The Magyars** were a people who lived from 3000 to 800BC on the steppes near Russia's river Don.

- **In 889,** the Magyars had been driven to the edge of their land by a people called the Pechenegs, so they were grateful for Arnulf's call.

- **Led by** the legendary Arpad, the Magyars swept into Hungary and made it their home.

- **In 975,** Arpad's great-grandson, Géza, became a Christian and began to form the Magyars into the Hungarian nation.

- **Géza's** son, Stephen (997-1038), carried on his work and became the first king of Hungary.

- **King Stephen,** also called St Stephen, was crowned by the pope on Christmas Day, AD1000.

▲ *King Stephen is a famous figure in Hungarian history and his crown became the symbol of the nation.*

201

Famous villains

- **Ancient history** has many famous villains – but most were called villains by their enemies, so we can never be sure just how bad they were.

- **Many of the** best-known villains are Roman, including the emperors Caligula and Nero and Sejanus, Emperor Tiberius's minister, who is believed to have poisoned Drusus, Tiberius's son.

- **The Emperor** Claudius's wife Messalina (AD22-48) got Claudius to execute any man who resisted her advances.

- **Claudius's** fourth wife, his niece Agrippina (AD15-59), probably poisoned him to make way for her son, Nero.

- **Many stories** are told of the Chinese emperor Shi Huangdi's cruelty, including his killing of 460 scholars.

- **Artaxerxes** (died 338BC) was the cruel Persian king who ravaged Egypt in 343BC.

▲ *Emperor Nero is painted as a corrupt villain of ancient Rome, blamed for the Great Fire of Rome in AD64.*

- **Artaxerxes** and all his sons but Arses were murdered by his minister Bagoas in 338BC. Bagoas then killed Arses and tried to poison the next king, Darius III. Darius found out and made Bagoas drink the poison himself.

- **Herod the Great** (73-4BC) of Judea (modern Israel) was a strong king, but he is known best for the murder of his beloved wife Mariamne in a jealous rage and the biblical tale of the 'Slaughter of the Innocents'. This tale relates how Herod ordered soldiers to kill all babies in Bethlehem in order to get rid of the infant Jews, who prophets had said would be a threat to him.

- **Pontius Pilate** (AD36) was the Roman governor of Judea who allowed Jesus to be crucified.

- **Theodora, wife of** Justinian I, was notorious for her secret police.

▶ *The Roman emperor Caligula was malicious and mentally unstable, striking terror wherever he went.*

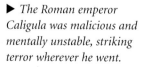

Early English kings

- **Egbert,** king of Wessex from AD802 to 839, became in effect the first king of England when he conquered Mercia at Ellandun in 829. But his rule lasted just a year before the Mercian king, Wiglaf, claimed Mercia back.

- **For 100 years,** much of England was lost to the Danes, but Alfred the Great's son Edward and his daughter Aethelflaed gradually drove the Danes out by 918.

- **England's** kingship really began with Athelstan, crowned 'King of all Britain' at Kingston on September 4, 925.

- **'Ethelred** the Unready' was king of England 978-1013 and 1014-1016. *Rede* was old English for advice, and his name meant he was always badly advised.

- **Ethelred** created so much distrust among his subjects that the Danes easily reconquered England in 980.

- **In 1013,** Dane Sweyn Forkbeard became king of England.

- **When** Sweyn died, Ethelred made a comeback until Sweyn's son, Canute, drove him out. Canute became king of England in 1016 by marrying Ethelred's widow, Emma.

▲ *King Canute*

- **Canute** ruled well. A story tells how he rebuked flatterers by showing how even he could not stop the tide coming in.

- **After Canute,** in 1035, came Harold I (1035–40, followed by Harthacanute (1040–42). Ethelred's son, Edward the Confessor, then became king – but the Danes did not want a Saxon king.

- **The Danes** called on their Norwegian allies, led first by Magnus then Harold Hardraada, to win back the throne.

▶ *The city of Winchester in southern England was Alfred the Great's capital, and in his time it became a great centre of learning. Canute also made it his capital, and his son Hardecanute is buried here, with Alfred.*

The first Scots

- **The first settlers** came to Scotland around 7000 years ago, and the remains of their huts can be seen on Skara Brae in Orkney.

- **People** called Picts arrived here shortly before the times of the Romans, who failed to conquer Scotland.

- **The Picts** may have come from the Black Sea region. They got their name from the tattooed pictures on their bodies.

- *Brochs* are 15-m-high stone towers built for defence around 100BC by ancestors of the Picts.

- **Celts** called Scots came from Dalriada in Ireland in *c.*470. They soon conquered the west.

- **After St Columba** came to set up Iona monastery in 563, Scotland was slowly converted to Christianity.

- **In 563**, Scotland was split into four kingdoms: the Scots' Dalriada in the west; the Picts in the north; the Britons' Strathclyde in the southwest; and Bernicia or Lothian of the Angles in the east.

◀ *The Romans gave the Picts their name – picti is Latin for 'painted people', after the Picts' decorative body tattoos.*

206

- **In 685,** the Picts drove out the Angles, and in 843, the Dalriada king, Kenneth McAlpin, conquered the Picts to create a country called Alba, the first Scotland.

- **In the 900s** and 1000s, many people fought to be king in Scotland. Kenneth III killed Constantine III to become king. Malcolm II killed Kenneth III and Duncan I who followed him was killed by his general, Macbeth. Macbeth was killed by Malcolm III.

- **Malcolm III's** wife was Saint Margaret (1045-1093), brought up in Hungary where her father was in exile.

▶ *Macbeth (died 1057) was the Scottish king who became the basis for Shakespeare's tragedy* Macbeth. *The real Macbeth killed Duncan in battle, not in his bed as in Shakespeare's famous play.*

207

Index

Index

Index

Index

Index

Index

Old Assyrian Empire 60
Old Babylonian Empire 42
Old Kingdom *40*, 41
Old Stone Age 20
Old Testament *58*
Olduvai Gorge, Tanzania 10
oligarchs 84, 85
olives 101, 126, 154
Olmecs **54-55**, *54*, 97
Olympians 106, *107*
Olympias, queen 108
Olympic Games 75
Omo Basin, Ethiopia 16
opposable thumb 10
oracle bones 45
ores 22, 24, 25, 45, 144
origins of mankind **8-9**
Orkney 206
ornaments 22
Osiris 52
ostraca 47
Ostria *121*
Ostrogoths 158
Otto I, king 188
outriggers *104*, 105
ovens 100

P

Pacific Islands 62, 196
Pacific Ocean 104
Pakistan 36, 132
Palaeolithic Period 20

Paleo-Indians 96
Palestine 58, 101, 116, 152
Panhellenic Games 75
Pannonia, Hungary 196
Papua New Guinea 30
papyrus 47, *47*, 65, *123*, 165
Paranthropus boisei 11
Paris, France 42, 183
Paris, Prince 73
Parthenon, Greece *85*, 98
passage graves 136
Pataliputra, India 132
patriach 152
patricians 111
Paul 152
Pavlov, Czechoslovakia 164
peatbog man 24
Pechenegs 196
Pella, Macedonia 108
Pepin the Short 194
Pergouset, France 18
persecution of Christians 152
Persepolis, Persia 66, 67
Persia 56, 109, 168
Persian empire **66-67**, 69, 108
Babylon 43
Byzantium 154
clothes 165
kings 52, 200
Peru 30, 54

Phaestos 51
phalanx 88, *108*
pharaohs **52-53**, 144
Alexander the Great 108
Egyptian writing 47
Tutankhamun 70
Phidas of Greece 98
Phillip II, king of Macedonia 108
philosophers **92-93**, 108
Phoenicians 74, **102-103**, 180
Picts 206, *206*, 207
Pilate, Pontius 117, 201
Pindar 98
Plato 92, 93
Pliny 116
ploughs 30, 81, 86, 148
poets,
Anglo-Saxons 172
Barbarians 158
caliphs 186
Celts 147
China 156
Fujiwaras 170, *171*
Greek 98, 106
Guptas 140
Homer 94, 95
Ireland 136
Vikings 202
police 36, 133
polis 84, *85*
Polynesians **104-105**, 192

Pompeii *128*, 129, 164
Pompey, general 114, 138
popes 152, 188
popinae *100*
population growth 17, 24, 148
portal graves 136
potassium argon dating 29
potters' wheels *34*, 40
pottery,
archaeology *28*
Britain 148
cooking 100
Egyptian writing 47
Melanesia 62
Praetorian Guard 150
Praxiteles of Greece 98
preserving bodies 64
Preslav 174
Priam, king 82
priests 41, 52, 57, 67
printing 80, 156
Processional Way, Babylon 43
Proconsul 8
Procopius 154
provinces, Ireland 136
Ptolemy, general 112
Pueblo Bonito, North America 134
Pueblo Indians 134
Punic Wars 111
purple dye 58, 102, 164, 165
Pyramid Texts 65
pyramids,

Index

Index

Acknowledgements

The publishers would like to thank the following artists
for contributing to this book:

Richard Berridge, Vanessa Card, Nicholas Forder, Chris Forsey, Mike Foster,
Terry Gabbey, Richard Hook, John James, Roger Kent, Aziz Khan,
Kevin Madison, Janos Marffy, Roger Payne, Terry Riley, Martin Sanders,
Rob Sheffield, Peter Sarson, Guy Smith, Roger Stewart,
Studio Galante, Mike Taylor, Rudi Vizi, Mike White, John Woodcock

The publishers would like to thanks the following sources for the use of
their photographs:

CORBIS: Page 56 Lyndsey Hebberd; Page 171 Bass Museum of Art;
Page 189 Archivo IcongraficoSA

All other pictures from the Miles Kelly Archives